PROJECT RISK MANAGEMENT

A PROACTIVE APPROACH

The books in the Project Management Essential Library series provide project managers with new skills and innovative approaches to the fundamentals of effectively managing projects.

Additional titles in the series include:

Effective Work Breakdown Structures, Gregory T. Haugan

Project Planning and Scheduling, Gregory T. Haugan

Managing Project Quality, Timothy J. Kloppenborg and Joseph A. Petrick

Project Measurement, Steve Neuendorf

Project Estimating and Cost Management, Parviz F. Rad

Project Risk Management: A Proactive Approach, Paul S. Royer

MANAGEMENTCONCEPTS
www.managementconcepts.com

PROJECT RISK MANAGEMENT

A PROACTIVE APPROACH

Paul S. Royer

ſſſ
MANAGEMENTCONCEPTS

Vienna, Virginia

ſſ
MANAGEMENTCONCEPTS
8230 Leesburg Pike, Suite 800
Vienna, VA 22182
(703) 790-9595
Fax: (703) 790-1371
www.managementconcepts.com

Printed in the United States of America

Library of Congress Cataloging-in-Publication Data

Royer, Paul S., 1946-
    Project risk management: a proactive approach/Paul S. Royer
      p. cm.
    Includes bibliographical references and index.
    ISBN 1-56726-139-6 (pbk.)
    1. Project management. 2. Risk management. I. Title.
HD69.P7 R69 2001
                            2001049445

About the Author

Paul Royer is the founder of Proactive Risk Management, an information technology and management consulting firm in Olympia, Washington, specializing in project management, risk management, and quality assurance. He has more than 30 years of experience in the information systems industry, specifically in health care, government, and consulting. His background includes project management, risk management, quality assurance, systems development, data and process modeling, data warehousing, data administration, training and coaching, methodology development and implementation, business requirement definition, and process improvement. He has a BA in Computer Science from the University of California at Berkeley.

For more than five years, Paul has concentrated on the risk aspects of project management. He has published several articles with the Project Management Institute on this topic and has presented them at PMI® national symposiums.

Table of Contents

Preface

Experience has shown that risk management must be critical to project managers: Unmanaged or unmitigated risks are among the primary causes of project failure. What we know, we plan for—and we are successful more often than not. Without mitigation, however, risks will introduce chaos and failure into an otherwise well-planned and well-managed project. This book addresses the underlying process of successful risk management throughout a project's lifecycle. It provides practical, tested, proactive risk management techniques for the practicing project manager and risk management awareness for project stakeholders.

BACKGROUND

Managing a successful project is like walking the highwire—it is a complex balancing act fraught with competing distractions. The successful tightrope walker has years of practice and starts training on a "low" wire. Much attention is paid to the setting of the guy wires and support poles to provide a predictable tension to the highwire. Moreover, intense concentration is required to focus on the task at hand and to ignore the noisy crowds. A prospective tightrope walker who does not pay attention to these prerequisites is sure to fall.

Likewise, rare is the project manager who can deal with the inherent risks, distractions, and complexities of project management without detailed plans and processes. Unfortunately, many project managers do not approach risk management with the same rigor they apply to other project management processes (i.e., scope/change management, issue management, conflict resolution, or deliverable-based work breakdown development and scheduling).

Over time, many project managers learn to manage risk by denial, sidestepping, and attempting to shield themselves. They develop various patterns of behavior to fend off the impact of risk-based failure, such as:

- Adding non-justified contingency time, money, or resources to the project plan (i.e., "padding" the estimate)
- Pointing fingers and placing blame elsewhere
- Begging forgiveness and renegotiating scope when the "unknowable" occurs
- Taking shortcuts in quality assurance activities in an attempt to avoid risk impact or missing milestones
- Eliminating infrastructure deliverables (e.g., training, metadata documentation)
- Reacting with an "it's just one of those things" attitude and expecting the stakeholder to accept it.

The trouble with these behaviors is that they offer no opportunity for learning, so project managers repeat them.

All these behavior patterns are reactionary, lead to project failures, and serve to weaken the credibility and confidence of the project manager. However, there are proactive steps that a project manager can and should take to mitigate and minimize the impact of foreseeable risk-based failure.

The Project Environment

Before exploring the steps to successful project risk management, it is useful to examine the characteristics of some project environments. The project manager is selected from the ranks of successful "doers." Correspondingly, membership on a project team comes as a positive recognition of past work and success. It naturally follows that project team planning and environment perceptions are positively focused (i.e., the project manager and team members are optimistic, positive individuals who believe they can do anything, without regard to time or resources). This does not imply failure, because many projects are successfully completed by the "superhuman" heroics of a few individuals. Over-optimism, however, represents a "Pollyanna" management approach and can lead to disaster.

During the project proposal and planning phases, the project manager draws on personal experience, the project team, and the stakeholder community to develop a project plan. Generally, a series of brainstorming sessions is held to define goals and objectives, set the boundaries of the project (i.e., scope), quantify deliverables, develop a project lifecycle approach, and establish the timetable, milestones, budget, and resources. This is the point in the project lifecycle when the team should identify risks and develop mitigation strategies; however, these steps are often neglected. Reasons for not spending the time and energy to examine risks carefully include:

- Quantifying risks could lead to non-funding of the project.
- The stakeholder doesn't want to spend the time and energy.
- The stakeholder doesn't believe the risks are real.
- The stakeholder wants a simple plan.

Another underlying force is at work here. Sociological trends and current philosophies of team building emphasize the need to be positive—problems are opportunities, risks are challenges to be overcome, negative thoughts are socially suppressed. In this environment, emphasizing risk results in being labeled a negative thinker and non-contributor—almost a pariah. It's as if we've forgotten a basic survival instinct: risk aversion. Our evolution involved a systematic process of learning to avoid risks. For example, it is theorized that we first learned to stand upright so that we could see above the grasses, thereby avoiding predators and sighting food and shelter sources. Risk-averse behavior is a survival trait that we should remember, even in today's sophisticated civilization.

Who Should Read This Book?

Project Risk Management is for everyone associated with a project. The project management neophyte, grizzled veteran project manager, and project sponsors all can use this book to better understand and contend with risk. Most people consider risk management to be the responsibility of the project manager; however, unmanaged risk affects everyone involved with a project.

Contents of This Book

There are positive, proactive steps that a project manager can take to manage and reduce risk. This book focuses on the processes needed to classify and identify risks, measure their impact, develop strategies to mitigate them, and plan for appropriate contingencies to minimize their impact.

The risk management processes discussed herein follow the standard project management lifecycle as outlined in the Project Management Institute's (PMI) *A Guide to the Project Management Body of Knowledge (PMBOK® Guide)*, 2000 Edition. The *PMBOK® Guide* outlines how to manage risk in each project phase, from project initiation through closure. It provides a set of processes, which, if implemented consistently, will dramatically reduce project risk to manageable proportions.

This book includes the following chapters:

- **Chapter 1—Risk Management As a Process.** This chapter defines the overall process of risk management and where it fits into the project lifecycle as defined by PMI in the PMBOK® Guide.

- **Chapter 2—Initiation: Opportunity Assessment.** Chapter 2 outlines a process for performing an initial risk and opportunity analysis of a potential project. Management can use the results to prioritize project selection. Project managers can use the results as initial input to risk identification and response planning.
- **Chapter 3—Planning: Risk Management Planning.** This chapter details the process for completing a risk analysis of the project as part of the planning process, including risk identification, categorization, developing a mitigation strategy, and contingency planning.
- **Chapter 4—Execution: Project Risk Audit.** Chapter 4 defines a process for performing project risk audits throughout the life of a project as an additional quality control process. This audit technique examines implemented project management processes, which, if not properly executed, become the source of significant risk.
- **Chapter 5—Controlling: Risk Management.** This chapter focuses on a continuing risk management process using the outputs of the risk management plan produced during the planning phase.
- **Chapter 6—Closure: Risk Knowledge Transfer.** Chapter 6 outlines a knowledge management process for increasing organizational awareness of risk and sharing risk experiences to reduce future risk-based project failure.
- **Chapter 7—Program Risk Audit.** The last chapter describes a technique and process for assessing the "temporal health" of a program of multiple interrelated projects. The technique concentrates on the organizational elements of program management.

Format of Each Chapter

To ensure consistency and increase understanding, each chapter of this book (except Chapter 1) is presented in four main sections:
- Introductory paragraphs
- Execution of the process
  - Participants
  - Timetable
  - Process steps
  - Deliverables
- Explanatory material (as required)
- Concluding remarks.

Paul S. Royer

Acknowledgments

Writing a book is not a solo effort, so acknowledgements are in order. First I need to thank my family—my wife, Corrine, who gave me continual support and acted as my muse when I was blocked; and, my daughter, Plynlymon, who reviewed uncounted rewrites and helped me phrase things less academically.

I would also like to thank Dr. Ginger Levin and Cathy Kreyche, who were always available to answer my repetitive, naive questions about language and style. They provided me invaluable guidance concerning content and gave me many ideas on expanding on certain concepts.

The Project Management Institute's Risk Special Interest Group was gracious enough to allow me to include its Risk Management Lexicon in this book. For an up-to-date version of the lexicon, as well as an extensive reference list, I direct the reader to the Risk SIG Website: www.risksig.com.

Finally, but no less importantly, I must acknowledge my employer, CIBER, Inc. They provided encouragement for me to write the book and allowed me to use our internal project management methodology, e.Acceleration™, as a starting point for certain risk management processes (i.e., project opportunity assessment, risk identification and response planning, and continuing risk management).

CHAPTER 1

Risk Management As a Project Management Process

It must be remembered that there is nothing more difficult to plan, more doubtful of success, nor more dangerous to manage than the creation of a new system. For the initiator has the enmity of all who would profit by the preservation of the old institution and merely the lukewarm defense in those who would gain by the new ones.

—MACHIAVELLI

The art of project management consists of many processes. As defined by the Project Management Institute in the *PMBOK® Guide*, there are five essential project management processes, as shown in Figure 1-1. For reference, we define these processes simply as follows:

- **Initiating processes**—Obtaining commitment to begin a project
- **Planning processes**—Establishing a plan to accomplish the business need that the project addresses
- **Executing processes**—Coordinating the people and other resources assigned to the project
- **Controlling processes**—Ensuring achievement of project goals through monitoring and measuring progress so that remedial action can take place in a timely fashion
- **Closing processes**—formalizing completion of the project by acceptance of final deliverables, leading to an orderly project end.

OVERVIEW OF RISK MANAGEMENT PROCESSES

Before discussing how to manage risk, we must agree on a definition for the term. In the context of project management, we define *risk* as:

The potential events or circumstances that threaten the planned execution of the project.

This definition puts a totally negative context around the word *risk*. Others, such as the Project Management Institute, include the positive

FIGURE 1-1   *PMBOK® Guide* Project Management Processes

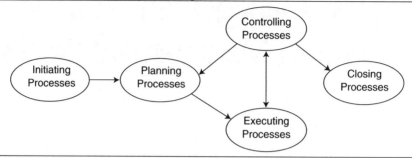

opportunities (impacts) that risks may have on a project. However, in developing a *proactive risk management* philosophy, it is most important to concentrate on the negative aspects of risk.

Each project management process has a corresponding risk management process, as shown in Figure 1-2. To establish a common reference framework, we define the risk management process simply as follows:

- **Initiation: Project opportunity assessment**—Examining the high-level requirements of the project opportunity to define risks versus opportunities in order to make a decision to proceed or not to proceed with the endeavor
- **Planning: Risk management planning**—Identifying risks and developing mitigation strategies and contingency plans to minimize their impact
- **Executing: Project risk audit**—Auditing the effectiveness of project management processes
- **Controlling: Continuing risk management**—Monitoring identified project risks to trigger the implementation of risk mitigation strategies and contingency plans; identifying new risks
- **Closure: Risk knowledge transfer**—Capturing lessons learned in the mitigation of project risks for use in future projects.

PROJECT OPPORTUNITY ASSESSMENT

As defined earlier, the project opportunity assessment examines the high-level requirements of the project opportunity to define risks, as opposed to opportunities, in order to make a decision to proceed or not to proceed with the endeavor. While particularly important to consulting organizations and subcontractors, this process is finding more and more applicability within enterprises that conduct their own projects. No one's resources are inexhaustible; therefore, it is critical to apply them to the "right" project. In addition to feasibility studies, return on investment analyses, and other strategies, the opportunity assessment provides additional insight to the decision-making process.

Process

The five steps in the opportunity assessment process are:
1. Assign opportunity assessor
2. Identify risks and opportunities
3. Evaluate risks and opportunities
4. Distribute opportunity assessment
5. Make go/no no decision.

FIGURE 1-2   Risk Management Processes

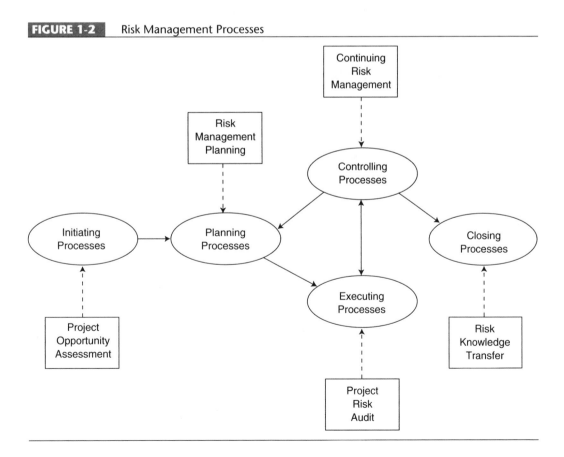

Risk Categories

The opportunity assessment process looks at nine assessment categories:
- Customer-associated
- Contract
- Project requirements
- Business practice expertise
- Project management
- Work estimates
- Project constraints
- Complexity and scale of deliverables
- Contractors.

Deliverable

The output from the opportunity assessment is a report that contains decision-making insight for management. A risk assessment of each category documents potential risks and assigns a risk rating on a simple low-medium-high scale. Likewise, the assessment documents potential opportunities (benefits) for each category.

RISK MANAGEMENT PLANNING

Following the decision to proceed with a project, detailed project planning begins. During this process, you must assess and mitigate potential risks to the project. Risk management planning is the process of identifying risks and developing mitigation strategies and contingency plans to minimize their impact. It involves all resources concerned in the enterprise (e.g., project manager, project team, stakeholders, technical support).

Project risks come in two types: *identifiable risks* and *unmanaged assumptions*:
- **Identifiable risks**—Risks identified during engagement contracting activities (i.e., project initiation) or during planning. For the most part, they are highly visible and immediately apparent to everyone (or at least someone) involved with the project.
- **Unmanaged assumptions**—Project assumptions that are not monitored to ensure continued validity. If an assumption fails to remain valid, it becomes a risk.

Process

Risk planning requires two sets of process steps after establishing a risk planning team: identifying risks and instituting assumption management.

These steps are:
1. Establish risk management planning team
2. Design identifiable risk planning
   2.1. Identify risks
   2.2. Categorize risks
   2.3. Prioritize risks
   2.4. Develop risk mitigation strategies
   2.5. Establish risk contingency plans
3. Begin assumption monitoring planning
   3.1. Identify assumptions
   3.2. Verify assumption validity
   3.3. Establish assumption monitoring metrics.

Risk Classification

To institute a consistent approach to risk management planning, we need a risk classification scheme. Numerous schemes are possible; as an enterprise matures in its management of risk, it will develop its own schema. The following are useful starting points:
1. Risk categories
   1.1. Scope/change management risk
   1.2. Operational risk
   1.3. Financial risk
   1.4. Project management risk
   1.5. Strategic risk
   1.6. Technology risk
   1.7. Failed assumption
2. Risk evaluation factors
   2.1. Risk severity
   2.2. Risk probability
   2.3. Risk timeframe
3. Risk mitigation strategies
   3.1. Risk acceptance
   3.2. Risk avoidance
   3.3. Risk protection
   3.4. Risk research
   3.5. Risk reserves
   3.6. Risk transfer

Adhering to a rigorous, consistent scheme for classifying risk may seem like overkill. However, if knowledge transfer concerning risk is an enterprise priority (and it should be), it is much simpler to classify risks during the risk planning process than to try to retrofit classification. (See Chapter 6, Closure: Risk Knowledge Transfer, for more information.)

Deliverables

The deliverables from this process establish risk management priorities and plans to be managed during the execution/control phases of the project. For risks of high impact or probability, the actual project plan and budget should reflect the cost and time of the mitigation strategy. Risk management planning deliverables include:
- Project risk worksheets
- Project assumption worksheets
- Risk management mitigation strategies included in the project plan.

PROJECT RISK AUDIT

Throughout the execution phase of a project, it is important to ensure that the project is generally healthy. A periodic project risk audit accomplishes this by assessing the effectiveness of project management processes. A risk audit should be performed by a project management professional who is as objective as possible. If stakeholders judge a project to be extremely important, an external risk auditor should be used.

Process

There are eight steps in the project risk audit process:
1. Identifying interviewees (project team, project manager, stakeholders)
2. Gathering evidence
3. Scheduling interviews
4. Conducting interviews
5. Analyzing evidence
6. Preparing findings
7. Preparing recommendations
8. Preparing report.

An initial risk audit takes from 20 to 70 hours over a 5- to 20-day period. Follow-up risk audits may take less time because they focus on prior audit recommendations and verification of continuing compliance to critical success factor (CSF) evidentiary requirements.

Critical Success Factors

Ten critical success factors are used to audit a project's compliance with industry best project management processes. Auditors also examine factors about the project's progress against plan and make a prognosis for successful completion. The ten CSFs are:

1. **Organization**—The project is appropriately organized.
2. **Risk management**—Project risks are identified and appropriately managed.
3. **Planning**—The project is appropriately planned.
4. **Milestones**—Project milestones are being met on schedule.
5. **Monitoring and control**—Project status is appropriately monitored and adequately controlled.
6. **Scope change control**—Project scope is appropriately controlled.
7. **Resources**—The project is appropriately resourced.
8. **Functional testing**—Appropriate functional acceptance-testing processes and plans are in place.
9. **Capacity and performance testing**—Appropriate capacity and performance acceptance testing processes and plans are in place.
10. **Training**—Appropriate and timely training is available.

Deliverables

Deliverables from the risk audit are used to inform both the project manager and stakeholders of risk findings and recommended corrective actions. The individual deliverables are:

- Risk audit summary
- Risk audit working papers
- Interview log
- Documentation log.

CONTINUING RISK MANAGEMENT

During the controlling phase of a project, the project manager must continuously manage risk using the risk management plan developed during the planning phase process. While project team members may have the responsibility for monitoring risk and assumption triggering metrics, the project manager is accountable for managing ongoing risk.

Process

There are three basic processes in continuing risk management:

1. **Monitoring identified risks**—Monitor the risk mitigation strategy

and contingency plan triggers established during the risk management planning process.

    1.1. Monitoring risk triggers

    1.2. Invoking risk management strategy

    1.3. Invoking risk management contingency plans

2. **Monitoring identified assumptions**—Monitor the assumption validity metrics established during the risk management planning process.

    2.1. Monitoring assumption validation triggers

    2.2. Invoking risk management planning process

3. **Identifying new risks**—Invoke the risk management planning process to deal with new risks or assumptions encountered during project execution.

In addition, we must invoke issue and scope change management processes to resolve risk-based issues and manage changes to project scope, resources, or schedule.

Deliverables

Continuing risk management involves executing the established risk management plan and accounting for newly discovered risks and assumptions. The following deliverables are necessary for properly documenting and communicating the effects of continuing risk management:

1. Risk management report

2. Updated risk management plan.

RISK KNOWLEDGE TRANSFER

Part of the closure phase of a project is recording lessons learned by evaluating the project and determining what went well and what could be improved next time. This is especially important relating to risk. The risk management planning process stresses the importance of *experience-based risk assessment*. While industry-based and general project risk lists may be relevant, the most important list to any enterprise is composed of the risks that it has encountered and what was successful in mitigating them. Therefore, it is critical that project closure reviews and documents the success of risk management.

Process

Molding risk knowledge transfer involves several steps:

1. Evaluating risk management success or failure
2. Documenting risk management success or failure
3. Cataloging and archiving risk management success or failure
4. Archiving risk management success or failure.

Deliverables

The primary deliverable from the risk knowledge transfer process is a summary of the success or failure of the executed risk management plan. While a simple paper or electronic repository of the risk and assumption management worksheets will serve this purpose, a repository of searchable data provides a more accessible and useful resource. This chapter outlines a simple database schema for storing the information.

PROGRAM RISK AUDIT

As enterprises focus outward and integrate across functional "silos," programs of interrelated projects become the norm. Managing these efforts properly requires a higher level of administration, often referred to as "program management." Like individual projects, programs can get into difficulties; therefore, a consistent process to review the ongoing health of programs is desirable.

A periodic program risk audit accomplishes this by assessing the effectiveness of organizational, communication, and management processes. It should be performed by an objective project management professional. If stakeholders judge a program critical to the success of the enterprise, an external risk auditor should be used.

Process

Similar to the project risk audit process, there are eight steps in the program risk audit process:
1. Identifying interviewees (program manager, stakeholders, project managers)
2. Gathering evidence
3. Scheduling interviews
4. Conducting interviews
5. Analyzing evidence
6. Preparing findings
7. Preparing recommendations
8. Preparing the report.

An initial risk audit should take from 60 to 120 hours over a 10- to 30-day period. Follow-up risk audits may take less time because they focus on prior audit recommendations and verification of continuing compliance to critical success factor evidentiary requirements.

Critical Success Factors

Ten critical success factors (CSFs) are used to audit a program's compliance with industry best standard program management processes. The auditors also examine factors about the program's progress against plan and prognosis for successful completion. The ten program CSFs are:

1. **Organization**—The enterprise is organized to meet its program goals and objectives, scaled to enterprise size.
2. **Planning**—The enterprise has planned for its program.
3. **Financial resources**—Sufficient financial resources (macro-level assessment) have been budgeted.
4. **Direction**—The enterprise is providing clear direction to its program and projects.
5. **Coordination**—The enterprise is coordinating its program efforts.
6. **Communication**—The enterprise is effectively communicating its program status and issues.
7. **Staffing resources**—The enterprise has devoted sufficient (macro-level assessment) program and technical staff to its program and projects.
8. **Control**—The enterprise is controlling its program and projects.
9. **Risk assessment**—The enterprise is fully aware of the program issues and risks.
10. **Seeks remedies**—The enterprise recognizes when it needs help and actively pursues remedies.

Deliverables

Deliverables from the risk audit are used to inform both the program manager and stakeholders of risk findings and recommended corrective actions. The individual deliverables are:

- Risk audit summary
- Risk audit working papers
- Interview log
- Documentation log.

This book provides a consistent framework and proactive approach for mitigating project risks. It complements and extends the risk management process defined by the Project Management Institute's *PMBOK®* Guide. The book follows the PMI-defined lifecycle of a project, so it can be used side by side with other project lifecycle references in a training environment or in the real world of project management.

The techniques and material provide different perspectives for different audiences:

- Acquaint the novice student of project management with the basics of project risk management
- Present extensions to traditional risk management concepts for the veteran project manager
- Demonstrate the practicality, necessity, and value of sound project risk management practices to project stakeholders and sponsors.

CHAPTER 2

Initiation: Project Opportunity Assessment

Life is short, the art long, opportunity fleeting, experiment treacherous, judgment difficult.

—HIPPOCRATES

The project initiation phase is the most important phase of a project. It is here that expectations are set with the stakeholder sponsor. Experience demonstrates that without clearly set expectations, projects are subject to a high rate of failure. Expectations relate to project scope, solution alternatives, preliminary plans, funding confines, temporal considerations, proposal creation, and proposal acceptance by the stakeholder. With these in place, most project managers assume that they should proceed directly to detailed planning.

The initiation phase, however, is the perfect place and time to conduct an initial risk and viability assessment, as shown in Figure 2-1. The Project Management Institute's *PMBOK® Guide* identifies the planning phase as the proper place for risk management planning. Nevertheless, the earlier you begin considering risk, the more likely you will be able to mitigate it successfully.

For consulting firms, there is another reason to do early project viability and risk assessment: deciding whether or not the project is worth pursuing at all. It is rare that consulting firms today can take on any sizeable project on an unlimited time and materials basis. Stakeholders want "fixed-price" contracts; what the stakeholders want, they will get. Consulting firms, therefore, need a consistent method for analyzing a prospective project and providing management sufficient information to decide whether or not to bid on the project.

Additionally, enterprises that have configured themselves into project organizations have the same need: to understand how to prioritize limited funds, personnel, and other resources to best align them with strategic priorities in order to choose the "right" projects.

FIGURE 2-1   Initiating Process and Project Opportunity Assessment

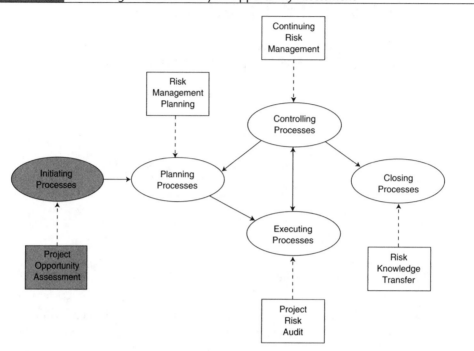

In both cases, a method is needed to examine prospective projects consistently and to decide whether to expend the "opportunity cost" required to develop an in-depth proposal. The method presented in this chapter meets this need. It will not, however, replace full feasibility studies, return on investment cost-benefit analyses, or prototype development.

EXECUTING A PROJECT OPPORTUNITY ASSESSMENT

A project opportunity assessment is a technique for performing a rapid analysis of relative project risks and opportunities. From this information, management gains valuable insight for making the "opportunity cost" commitment to complete and submit a proposal and to proceed with its planning and execution. Figure 2-2 illustrates the five steps in the opportunity assessment process.

Participants

If at all possible, the person executing the project opportunity assessment should not have a stake in the project outcome. No matter how objective we think we are, if we have a stake in an outcome, we are positively biased. This is only human nature, not a fault. Therefore, the assessment should not be performed by a salesperson, prospective project manager, prospective team

FIGURE 2-2 Opportunity Assessment Process Steps

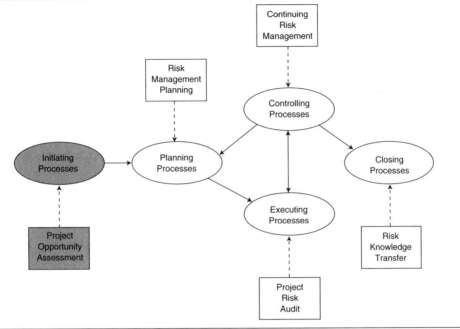

members, or stakeholders. The opportunity assessor draws on many parties to construct the assessment, as shown in Table 2-1.

If the project is internal to an enterprise, these people will include stakeholders, sponsors, technical infrastructure support staff, and anyone else with a stake in or concern about the project's outcome. Conversely, if the project is external to the proposed project team's enterprise (i.e., a contract

TABLE 2-1 Opportunity Assessment Participants

Participant	Involvement
Opportunity Assessor	• Plans and conducts the project opportunity assessment • Conducts interviews, if customer sponsor and stakeholders are available • Analyzes evidence (RFP), feasibility study, technology environment, etc.) • Prepares findings and recommendations • Presents opportunity assessment report
Proposed Project Manager	• Coordinates access to project team, sponsors, and stakeholders • Participates in risk/opportunity interviews • Gathers evidence for assessor
Sales/Account Executive (if applicable)	• Participate in risk/opportunity interview process
Subject Matter Experts	• Participate in risk/opportunity interview process • Prepare preliminary work effort estimates
Customer Sponsor	• Participates in risk/opportunity interview process, if available
Customer Stakeholders	• Participates in risk/opportunity interview process, if available

project opportunity), then access to stakeholders may be quite limited. In fact, access may be restricted to the request for proposal (RFP) document, public-forum vendor conferences, and questions submitted in writing to the RFP coordinator. In this case, it is even more important to perform an objective opportunity assessment.

Timetable

The opportunity assessment process is meant to be quick, as its only purpose is to help decide whether or not to proceed with proposal development and detailed project planning. While it may take several days to gather the necessary information, a knowledgeable assessor can complete the assessment in five to twenty hours. The assessment is based on nine risk/opportunity factors, as delineated in the Opportunity Assessment Risk/Opportunity Factors section. Table 2-2 outlines the effort and required time for a typical opportunity assessment.

Steps

The opportunity assessment process consists of five steps (see Figure 2-2). The assigned opportunity assessor conducts all the activities and prepares the go/no-go recommendation for management.

1. **Assigning the opportunity assessor**—Management assigns the position of opportunity assessor. As mentioned earlier, this person should be as objective and unbiased as possible, that is, he or she should have no vested interest in the outcome of the assessment. In addition, the assessor should be experienced in several disciplines:
   - Project management
   - Risk assessment
   - Deliverables and activities required to satisfy the opportunity's objectives.

2. **Identifying risks and opportunities**—By perusing requirements, interviewing appropriate stakeholders, and reviewing other related

TABLE 2-2 Project Opportunity Assessment Timetable

Task	Effort in Hours	Elapsed Time in Days
Assign opportunity assessor	~ 1	>½ – 1
Identify risks and opportunities	1 – 4	>½ – 3
Evaluate risks and opportunities	1 – 4	>½ – 1
Distribute opportunity assessment	1 – 4	>½ – 1
Make go/no go decision	1 – 4	>½ – 1
Total	5 – 20 hours	~2 – 7 days

documents, the assessor identifies potential risks and opportunities in the nine assessment risk/opportunity factors.

3. **Evaluating risks and opportunities**—After identifying the potential risks and opportunities, the assessor evaluates them and documents the results on an opportunity assessment worksheet. To aid in objective evaluation, guidelines are established for mandatory requirements for assigning a "low" risk to each factor.

4. **Distributing opportunity assessment**—The assessor distributes the completed opportunity assessment to enterprise management responsible for reviewing and approving the allocation of resources to project efforts. While the assessor makes the go/no-go recommendation, management bears the ultimate responsibility and accountability for allocating resources to a project.

5. **Making the go/no-go decision**—Management decides whether or not to expend further resources in developing proposals and plans for a project to meet the objectives of the opportunity. This is not an ultimate approval to do the project—just the approval to expend the "opportunity cost" necessary to estimate project costs accurately.

Project Opportunity Assessment and the "Small" Project

What is a "small" project?

By their nature, small projects are usually less risky than large projects. Consequently, it may seem like too much overhead to plan for and execute a formal project opportunity assessment. However, you must be careful in your definition of a "small" project. Each organization should establish a categorization scheme to help define small projects that should not require complete, formal project risk audits. Let's look at a couple of examples:

1. **Dollar Value:** To a $700 million-dollar-a-year revenue consulting firm, a $60,000 fixed-price project may be almost insignificant from a risk standpoint. Conversely, the same $60,000 project to a two-person firm may be critical to success and a positive balance sheet.

2. **Project Length:** A three-month engagement may seem small on the surface. However, if it were a 20-person effort, then it would hardly be small by almost anyone's criteria.

The message here is to deliberately examine all projects and decide which project management processes and practices are required to ensure success. Remember, project risk management is a standard project management process even if it is not often practiced.

In many instances, the decision to proceed with a project seems a foregone conclusion. That is, someone determines a need, provides funding, and authorizes the initiation of a project. This may seem very obvious for "small" projects. Nevertheless, as an opportunity assessment can be completed in as little as one hour's time, perform the exercise. If nothing else, the output from an opportunity assessment provides a starting point for risk identification and response planning.

Deliverables

A completed worksheet from an opportunity assessment is the basic deliverable (see Figure 2-3). The worksheet contains a description of the risks and opportunities for each assessment factor and a risk rating of low, medium, or high. It also contains the assessor's overall recommendation to proceed or not to proceed.

OPPORTUNITY ASSESSMENT RISK/OPPORTUNITY FACTORS

As mentioned earlier and shown in Figure 2-3, there are nine risk/opportunity factors that the assessor must evaluate using a straightforward, low-medium-high scale:

- **Low**—There is little threat to the project. The risk is unlikely to materialize; even if it does materialize, the impact on the project is relatively small.
- **Medium**—There is a significant chance that the project will suffer significant damage because of the outcome.
- **High**—The project will likely experience serious repercussions.

For each risk factor, there are rules (i.e., specific circumstances) to guide the assessor on conditions to be satisfied in order to assign a "low" rating. In addition, the assessor needs to document the perceived risks and opportunities for each factor.

Customer-Associated Risks

There are three customer-associated risks:

1. The customer will not be efficient, effective, or complete in meeting its obligations to the project.

| FIGURE 2-3 | Opportunity Assessment Worksheet |

Risk category	Risk Rating	Risk Comments	Opportunity Comment
1. Customer-associated Risks			
2. Contract Risks			
3. Requirements Risk			
4. Proposed Project Team Experience Risk			
5. Project Management Risk			
6. Work Estimate Risk			
7. Project Constraints Risk			
8. Complexity and Scale of Deliverables Risk			
9. Contractors Risk			
Recommendation			

2. The users are insufficiently available or insufficiently knowledgeable to affect the requirements and testing.
3. The users have unrealistic expectations about the outcome of the project.

Rules

- The assessor may not assign a "low" rating unless the customer has committed to a strong and timely decision-making process.
- The assessor may not assign a "low" rating unless the customer project manager and the key customer decision makers are reasonably experienced in their roles.
- The assessor may not assign a "low" rating if there is any history of past difficulties or poor communications of a material nature between the business practice and the customer.
- The assessor may not assign a "low" rating if there is any reason to doubt the competency of customer team members or the quality of components that will be provided by the customer.
- The assessor may not assign a "low" rating if there are known difficulties in identifying appropriate users.

Contract Risks

Contract risks arise from the possibility that the potential contract will contain clauses obligating the business practice to terms or conditions that are unreasonably costly to meet. These terms may include performance penalties, contract termination penalties, and warranty holdbacks.

Rules

- The assessor may rate this risk as "low" only if the contract provides suitable relief for at-risk scenarios in the event that the customer does not meet its project responsibilities.
- The assessor may rate this risk as "low" only if the contract provides a clear and reasonable process for certifying that deliverables comply with the contract. At a minimum, the customer must put in writing any reasons for its non-acceptance of a deliverable, and the contract should include a default acceptance if the customer does not provide such a document within a specified period.

Requirements Risk

This is the risk that the requirements analysis will never reach a point that allows confidence that project deliverables are completely defined.

Rule
- The assessor may not rate this risk as "low" if there are known issues or events that threaten to change requirements significantly after the initial requirements gathering sessions are concluded.

Proposed Project Team Experience Risk

This is the risk that the proposed project team lacks personnel with experience in designing or implementing major deliverables.

Rules
- The assessor may not rate this risk as "low" if members of the project team have not previously implemented any significant final deliverable.
- The assessor may not rate this risk as "low" if specific employee names must be included in the contract.
- The assessor may not rate this risk as "low" if employees are needed for a specialized skill who have not been hired or identified.
- The assessor may not rate this as risk "low" if more than 40 percent of the intended project team staff has less than a year of experience with the intended project deliverables.

Project Management Risk

There is a risk that the intended project manager will lack appropriate experience and training.

Rules
- The assessor may not rate this risk as "low" unless there is a reasonable expectation that the assigned project manager will have significant project management experience.
- The assigned project manager also must have sufficient subject matter expertise, familiarity with requirements gathering methods, project planning skills, and experience or training in using change control and issues tracking procedures.

Work Estimate Risk

There is a risk that the work effort is poorly estimated.

Rules
- The assessor must rate this risk as "high" if there has been significant pressure on the estimator to provide low or optimistic work estimates.

- The assessor may not rate this risk as "low" if the estimator is inexperienced in estimating the work called for by this project.

Project Constraints Risk

There is a risk that uncommon constraints on the design, implementation, or work environment will lead to greater expense, a longer schedule, or a decrease in the quality of the deliverables.

Rule

- The assessor may not rate this risk as "low" if the proposal is referenced by the contract.

Complexity and Scale of Deliverables Risk

There is a risk that the required deliverables will be of such complexity or scale that the degree of difficulty will increase and pose delays and cost overruns.

Rule

- The assessor may not rate this risk as "low" if the proposed project requires untried or "bleeding-edge" technology.

Contractors Risk

There is a risk that the proposed project team will be potentially responsible for the performance of a third-party contractor who is not sufficiently committed to the project's success, rules, or procedures.

Rule

- The assessor may not rate this risk as "low" if there is a contractor (either a primary or subcontractor) with substantial participation on the project.

A formal opportunity assessment process may be new to many enterprises. However, as organizations move toward being project-oriented, they need to respond quickly. Enterprise resource allocation thus becomes critical. The opportunity assessment process described here will provide enterprises with a more consistent, improvable process for selecting the right projects.

Remember that the result of the assessment is a very high-level risk and opportunity assessment. The assessor's recommendation to proceed or not to proceed is only one factor in selecting projects for funding. A negative recommendation is not ironclad; it is just one more piece of information to aid decision makers. If a high-risk opportunity is undertaken, then the assessment results become one more piece of information to feed into the risk management planning process.

CHAPTER 3

Risk Management Planning

*Regret for the things we did can be tempered by time; it is regret for the
things we did not do that is inconsolable.*

—SYDNEY J. HARRIS

Risks are inherent in every project. There is no avoiding them; therefore, you
must make plans to manage risk and minimize its impact on the project. Risk
response planning occurs during the project planning process, as illustrated
in Figure 3-1.

EXECUTING RISK MANAGEMENT PLANNING

Risk management planning deals with two types of risks: *identifiable
risks* and *unmanaged assumptions. Identifiable risks* are those that can be
recognized during planning and engagement contracting activities. For the
most part, they are highly visible and immediately apparent to everyone (or
at least someone) involved with the project. In contrast to identifiable risks,
unmanaged assumptions are neither visible nor apparent as risks and can be
the most dangerous.

Planning for both is a straightforward process. You must identify risks
and plan how to handle them; to be complete, you need to analyze the
project's assumptions to ensure that they do not lead to unplanned risks.

Participants

While the project manager is usually charged with risk management, he
or she does not function in a vacuum. Everyone involved in the project—the
project manager, project team, customer stakeholders, sponsors, and subject
matter experts—should have input into risk management planning. Table 3-1
outlines the risk management planning participants and their involvement.

FIGURE 3-1   Planning Process and Risk Management Planning

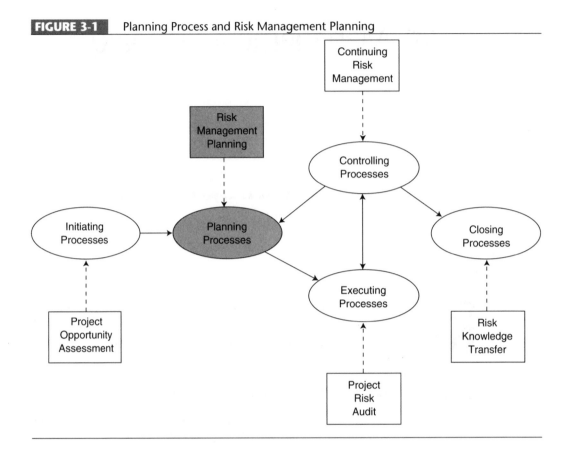

Timetable

The breadth and depth of risk management planning depend on the scope of the project and its inherent risks. If the type of project being planned

TABLE 3-1   Risk Management Planning Participants

Participant	Involvement
Project Manager	• Coordinates access to project team, stakeholders, and other subject matter experts • Facilitates risk planning activities • Prepares and documents risk management plans
Project Team (including external vendors or subcontractors)	• Participate in risk planning process
Subject Matter Experts	• Participate in risk planning process
Sponsor	• Participates in risk planning process
Stakeholders	• Participate in risk planning process

is new to the enterprise and the scope is large, then it necessarily follows that risk planning will require significant time. Conversely, if the project type is well understood and there are past successes, risk planning may need very little time. However, risk planning is serious business and is not to be taken lightly, regardless of the size of the project. Table 3-2 outlines the activities, suitable effort times, and elapsed times for most projects.

Steps

There are two parallel paths through the risk management planning process: risk planning and assumption planning (see Figure 3-2). The first step in the process is to establish a risk management planning team. After establishing the team, there is a five-step process for identifiable risk planning and a similar three-step process to build assumption management plans.

1. **Establish risk management planning team**—In many cases, the project manager takes responsibility for risk management planning. However, this in itself is a risk. No one individual can or should assume that he or she can effectively identify and deal with all risks. Spreading the risk management planning responsibility among several individuals reduces risk and ensures a more comprehensive risk management plan. In addition, including stakeholders and sponsors in risk management planning ensures that risk mitigation strategies and contingency plans will be properly accounted for in the budget. During planning, the project manager, team, and appropriate sponsors and stakeholders establish a risk management planning team.

TABLE 3-2 Risk Management Planning Timetable

Task	Effort in Hours	Elapsed Time in Days
Establish risk management planning team	1 – 4	>½ – 1
Identify risks	1 – 4	>½ – 1
Categorize risks	1 – 4	>½ – 1
Prioritize risks	1 – 4	>½ – 1
Develop risk mitigation strategies	1 – 8	>½ – 1
Establish risk contingency plans	1 – 4	>½ – 1
Identify assumptions	1 – 4	>½ – 1
Verify assumption validity	1 – 4	>½ – 1
Establish assumption monitoring metrics	1 – 4	>½ – 1
Total	9 – 40 hours	~2 – 9 days

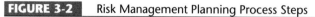

FIGURE 3-2   Risk Management Planning Process Steps

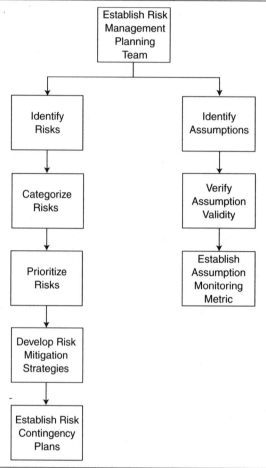

This team identifies, categorizes, and prioritizes risks to the project. Using this information, it develops and employs risk mitigation strategies and contingency plans to manage the risk.

2. **Plan for identifiable risks—**

   2.1. **Identify risks—**Risk identification is a heuristic process. Two of the most effective techniques are experience and brainstorming (see Techniques section). Whatever technique is used, the risk management team identifies the risks and begins documenting them.

   2.2. **Categorize risks—**After identifying potential risks, the next step is to categorize them so they may be assigned priorities later. Categories are very useful for future analysis and risk planning efforts. While each enterprise must establish its own scheme, this chapter defines seven useful risk categories.

2.3. **Prioritize risks**—Following categorization, it is necessary to prioritize risks in terms of their severity and probability. This two-dimensional prioritization, together with estimates of risk timeframe, provides the parameters for establishing risk mitigation strategies and contingency plans.

2.4. **Develop risk mitigation strategies**—Mitigation strategies to minimize risks are now developed and documented. For sufficiently severe, probable, or near-term risks, these plans and the resources required should be included in the baseline project plan, with budget and other resources allocated. Address lesser severity and probable risks with contingency funding and close monitoring during project execution. (See Chapter 4—Controlling: Continuing Risk Management.)

2.5. **Establish risk contingency plans**—While risk mitigation strategies are necessary to minimize risk impact, they are often insufficient. That is, risk mitigation strategies themselves can fail. Therefore, for the highest impact and probable risks, you should develop contingency plans at this point to monitor risk mitigation strategy and remedy any failure.

3. **Plan for assumption management**—Many assumptions are made during the project planning phase. Unfortunately, failed assumptions become risks if not properly managed.

3.1. **Identify assumptions**—Project planning relies on assumptions, which require documentation by the risk management planning team for future reference and verification.

3.2. **Verify assumption validity**—Verify that all project planning assumptions are valid. Manage invalidated assumptions as new project risks.

3.3. **Establish assumption monitoring metric**—Establish a monitoring metric for each high-impact project assumption. This will allow monitoring during the execution of the project to ensure continued assumption validity.

Deliverables

Risk management planning produces several deliverables that document the strategies and contingency plans to mitigate risks and to ensure that assumptions do not become risks. The risk management planning output

---

Risk Planning and the "Small" Project

It can be argued that the detailed risk planning technique described here is overkill and too burdensome for a "small" project. Nevertheless, a discerning project manager will not underestimate the impact of risk on any project. Often, a small effort can get into more trouble than a large one because customer expectations allow for little if any contingency time or budget.

If the project team has a high degree of understanding about the project's deliverable scope and techniques to produce the deliverables, then effort estimates will have a high degree of confidence. This naturally results in a project plan and budget with an expected high degree of accuracy. In this case it may be well justified to shorten the risk planning process; however, one note of caution: *Beware of unmanaged assumptions!*

---

also modifies the baseline project plan by inserting activities and deliverables called for by the risk planning effort. The basic deliverables are:

1. **Project risk worksheet**—Documents risks, their categorization, risk mitigation strategy, and contingency plans. See Figure 3-3 for an example of a risk worksheet.

2. **Project assumption worksheet**—Document assumptions and the monitoring metric used to ensure continued validity. See Figure 3-4 for an example of an assumption worksheet.

3. **Updated project plans**—Document activities and deliverables added to the baseline project plan to account for high severity and probability risks and their mitigation strategies.

RECOGNIZABLE RISK DEFINITION AND PLANNING TECHNIQUES

As stated earlier, recognizable risks are those that can be identified during planning and engagement contracting activities. For the most part, they are highly visible and immediately apparent to everyone (or at least someone) involved with the project. Typical examples include new technology, financial resource constraints, staff resource limitations, and changes to business processes. Historically, mitigation strategies have often been put in place to handle these kinds of risks.

Unfortunately, mitigation strategies can introduce risks of their own. For example, if the project calls for the introduction of new technology, training could be included in the project plan as a risk mitigation strategy. However, while training is necessary to acquire new skills, it is usually not sufficient. That is, coaching, mentoring, or the ready availability of an experienced

FIGURE 3-3   Risk Worksheet

Project Risk Worksheet			
Project Information			
ID:		**Manager:**	
Customer:			
Title:			
Risk Definition			
ID:		**Definition Date:**	
Title:			
Description:			
Accountable Person:			
Underlying Assumption:			
Category:	**Severity:**	**Probability:**	**Timeframe:**
Monitoring Metric:			
Risk Mitigation Strategy Definition			
Strategy Type:			
Strategy Title:			
Strategy:			
Implementation Date:			
Success Metric:			
Estimated Cost:		**Actual Cost:**	
Measure: Success ☐ Failure ☐		**Measure Date:**	
Success/Failure Description:			
Risk Mitigation Contingency Plan Definition			
Contingency Title:			
Contingency Plan:			
Trigger:			
Estimated Cost:		**Actual Cost:**	
Implementation Date:			
Measure: Success ☐ Failure ☐		**Measure Date:**	
Success/Failure Description:			

practitioner is often required to ensure skill transfer and proficiency in a short period. Therefore, it would be advisable to include a contingency plan for an onsite expert or consultant, should the need arise.

It follows that as risks are identified, a risk mitigation plan should be developed and implemented. Further, a contingency plan should be included for high risks, with a triggering circumstance or measure defined to invoke it. It may not be necessary to plan the contingency action in detail at this time; however, it is important to know what should be planned based on an appropriate trigger (i.e., a set of warning signs). Continuing the new

| FIGURE 3-4 | Assumption Worksheet |

Project Assumption Worksheet		
Project Information		
ID:	Manager:	
Title:		
Assumption Definition		
ID:	Definition Date:	
Title:		
Description:		
Accountable Person:		
Category:		
Assumption Verified By:	Verification Date:	
Assumption Measurement		
Success Metric:		
Measure: Success ☐ Failure ☐		
Success/Failure Description:		
Potential Mitigation Strategy Definition		
Strategy:		
Conversion to Risk Information		
Trigger:		
Risk Id:		
Risk Title:		
Implementation Date:		

technology risk example, if anticipated productivity measures are not met, the expert is made available.

Risk mitigation strategies and contingency plans cost time, money, and resources to develop and implement. Rare would be the project in which every risk was manifested and every contingency plan triggered. In addition, project sponsors often do not want to spend the time (i.e., money) for detailed risk mitigation planning. Consequently, it may be more appropriate to set an overall risk mitigation budget as a percentage of the overall projected costs rather than to cost in detail each identified risk's mitigation strategy and contingency plan. Industry experience suggests a 5 percent contingency budget for identifying and tracking risks. Adding another 5 percent risk mitigation contingency budget to deal with unanticipated risks would be prudent.

Risk Identification Techniques

To manage risks properly, you must first "discover" them. Two common techniques for accomplishing this are experience-based and brainstorming-based risk assessment.

Experience-Based Risk Assessment

The mark of a successful project manager (i.e., one who can survive both organizationally and personally) is the ability to learn from experience. The impact of unmitigated risks encountered in past projects should be imprinted indelibly in the psyche of the project manager. Best practice risk management ensures the availability of this information by building a risk knowledgebase. (See Chapter 6—Closure: Risk Knowledge Transfer.)

Using the risk knowledgebase, the risk management planning team examines the cataloged risks and assesses their applicability to the project. If applicable, the team adds them to the project risk list to be cataloged and prioritized.

Brainstorming-Based Risk Assessment

Facilitated brainstorming sessions with customer stakeholders, project team members, and infrastructure support staff are the primary techniques used here to define risks and their mitigation strategies and contingency plans. The process defines risks in one column, mitigating strategies in a second, and potential contingency plans in a third, making it easy to determine where the organization is exposed to an unmitigated risk. This form of facilitated session is also known as "force field analysis."

Table 3-3 provides a minimal example of this technique. As can be seen in the example, the brainstorming session can identify multiple mitigation strategies or contingency plans for a risk.

Risk Classification

In the real world, there is not enough money, time, or resources to deal with all risks; management must select the risks for which to develop and implement mitigation and contingency strategy plans. It is therefore important to develop an objective approach for classifying risks and establishing priorities. One approach that has proven successful is examining each risk and classifying it according to the following four factors:

1. Category of risk
2. Severity or impact on the successful completion of a project milestone

TABLE 3-3　Example of Risk vs. Strategy and Contingency Plan Analysis

Risk	Mitigation Strategy	Contingency Plan
Lack of available project management skill	• Hire experienced project managers	• Establish project office and assign staff as aide to project manager
	• Provide project management training	• Provide project management mentors and coaching
Lack of skilled resources for programming	• Train staff	• Provide skill mentors and coaching
	• Hire skilled staff	• Contract for missing skills
	• Re-prioritize skilled staff efforts to align with strategic objectives	• Hire additional skilled staff
Too long between deliverables	• Create interim milestones	• Review significance of the deliverables. If they're worth the effort, then move them forward. If they should be delayed for some measurable time, then they should not be part of the project.
Cutting-edge, demanding technical effort	• Create series of technical prototypes and "prove as you go"	• Reduce complexity of technical architecture • Increase temporal scope (i.e., time frame) of project

3. Probability or likelihood
4. Timeframe.

Risk Categories

Predefining risk categories provides a way to classify risks for inclusion in the organizational knowledgebase. While every organization should establish its own risk categories based on its special needs, the following are seven useful risk categories:

- **Scope/change management risk**—The risk that project scope is not well defined or will change during project execution
- **Operational risk**—The risk that project failure will affect the operations of the enterprise
- **Financial risk**—The risk that project failure will negatively affect enterprise financial resources or that insufficient financial resources will be available to complete the project successfully
- **Project management risk**—The risk that poor project management will negatively affect project success
- **Strategic risk**—The risk that project failure will have a negative impact on enterprise strategy
- **Technology risk**—The risk that project reliance on new, "bleeding-edge" technology will negatively affect project success or that project team experience with the proposed technology is insufficient

- **Failed assumption**—The risk that invalid assumptions will negatively affect project success.

Within any organization, certain risk categories may represent higher risks for project failure. For example, some organizations may have substantial experience introducing new technology and therefore will understand how to deal with technology risks. On the other hand, another organization that has not introduced new technology for some time may need to be especially careful when doing so.

It follows that the risk categories themselves may have weighting factors assigned to modify the severity/probability risk factor ratings. Such weighting factors may be helpful when quantifying overall project risk, but they are no substitute for proper risk mitigation strategy and contingency planning.

Risk Severity

Risk severity relates to the impact on the project and business if the risk manifests itself, and it should be rated for objective evaluation. While more complex numerical severity rating schemes can be defined, it is often sufficient to use a simple high-medium-low scale, defined as follows:

- **High**—Without mitigation, project objectives are in jeopardy.
- **Medium**—Without mitigation, a deliverable/milestone is at risk.
- **Low**—No deliverable/milestone is currently at risk, but an issue bears watching and is a candidate for active mitigation.

Risk Probability

Risk probability is often indicated by a faulty assumption of resource and skill availability or by a timing and synchronization issue. As with risk severity, a simple high-medium-low rating scale is usually sufficient for objective evaluation:

- **High**—Without mitigation and monitoring, the project deliverable/milestone completion will interrupt the project's critical path.
- **Medium**—Without mitigation and monitoring, project deliverable/milestone completion will enter the project critical path.
- **Low**—No project deliverable/milestone is at risk unless delays become excessive; therefore, risk should be documented and monitored.

Risk Timeframe

Risk timeframe analyzes when risk can be expected to occur. Obviously, the sooner the risk could occur, the more detailed your planning should be. For the purpose of analysis, another three-point scale is useful:

- **High**—Within the next two weeks

- **Medium**—Two weeks to two months from current date
- **Low**—More than two months from current date.

These values are only suggestions and will need to be tailored for each enterprise and possibly each project. They will need to be adjusted as time passes, until the risk has occurred or the likelihood of it occurring has disappeared.

Risk Mitigation Strategy and Contingency Plan Evaluation and Planning

Combining the risk severity and probability factors leads to the matrix of risk severity versus probability (see Table 3-4), which can aid in defining when to prepare risk mitigation strategies and contingency plans. For example, a risk with high severity but low probability gives a severity/probability rating (SPR) of 2 and calls for a fully developed risk mitigation strategy and outlined contingency plan.

More detailed and sophisticated matrices are being used by many companies and are contained in many project management software support tools. However, significant results can be achieved with this minimal level of complexity. As well as quantifying risk severity and risk probability, other objective measures of risk should be considered—that is, where possible, the degree of impact on cost, schedule, and deliverable quality should be examined and quantified.

As indicated, Table 3-4 provides an objective starting point for prioritizing risks:

1. Examine all risks with either a high severity or probability in detail (i.e., severity/probability factor rating [SPR] of 2 or 3). Develop a risk mitigation strategy, and include it in the project plan and budget.

Table 3-4	Risk Severity vs. Probability Factor Matrix		
High	2	2	3
Medium	1	1	2
Low	0	1	2
Severity Factor	Low	Medium	High
		Probability Factor	

Severity/Probability Factor Rating (SPR)
3   mitigation strategy and detailed contingency plan
2   mitigation strategy and outlined contingency plan
1   mitigation strategy
0   treat as a project assumption

2. If both the severity and probability factors are high (i.e., SPR of 3), develop a detailed contingency plan with budget.

3. If only one factor is high (i.e., SPR of 2), then it is probably appropriate to outline a contingency strategy with a trigger and leave the planning details until the trigger is activated.

4. For areas with at least a medium severity or probability (i.e., SPR of 1), develop a risk mitigation strategy. Then, prepare a detailed contingency plan if monitoring shows an increase in risk during the project.

5. Establish a metric to allow monitoring for those risks with both a low severity and probability (i.e., SPR of 0). Treat those risks as a project assumption and deal with them in the same manner (see Assumption Definition and Management Techniques).

6. Consider the timeframe of the risk carefully at this point. In addition, ensure that the timeframe is monitored closely during the controlling phase of project execution to minimize risk impact and allow proper time for mitigation.

Risk Mitigation Categories

Another useful quantification of risk is mitigation strategy. Categorizing risk mitigation strategy allows another indexing of risks for future reference. (See Chapter 6—Closure: Risk Knowledge Transfer.) The following are six useful mitigation strategy categories:

1. **Risk acceptance**—Address it if and when it happens; used if consequences are limited.

2. **Risk avoidance**—Eliminate the specific threat or reject an approach because risk is too great and no acceptable means of resolving it can be found.

3. **Risk protection**—Use insurance and redundancy to mitigate the risk.

4. **Risk research**—Obtain more information. Prototyping is a typical research tactic, as are volume testing and increasing throughput.

5. **Risk reserves**—Create contingencies in the project schedule and budget in anticipation of projected risk impacts.

6. **Risk transfer**—Transfer risk to another group when it has the necessary authority or control.

After developing mitigation and contingency strategies for the risks, the project manager and the assigned accountable person are responsible for providing continuous monitoring and risk status evaluation during project execution. For effective monitoring, a success measurement for the mitigation strategy and a triggering event that identifies when the contingency plan will be invoked must be identified and tracked. In addition, the project manager, team members, and stakeholders should be alert for new risks throughout the lifecycle of the project.

Documenting Risks

Figure 3-3 presented a possible format for recording risks, their underlying assumptions, mitigation strategies, and contingency plans. Transforming this into a database format provides an even more automated method of capturing the risk management data and an easy vehicle for reporting and administration. (See Chapter 6—Closure: Risk Knowledge Transfer for a description of a risk management knowledgebase.)

An alternative to the full risk worksheet is a spreadsheet (see Figure 3-5). While it cannot capture as much information, a spreadsheet may suffice for a small project in which scope, deliverables, and work effort are well understood.

Aggregating Individual Project Risks

It would seem logical to add the individual risks, calculate the average risk, and then assign that risk to the project as a whole. As long as you do not include the low-risk items, this is probably a safe estimate. However,

FIGURE 3-5   Risk Spreadsheet

	A	B	C	D	E	F	G	H	I	J	K
1		Customer									
2		Project Title									
3		Project Manager									
4											
5	Id. #	Description of Risk	Prob-ability	Severity	Time-frame	Identified By	Date Identified	Mitigation Strategy	Owner	Risk Occurred	Mitigation Outcome
6											
7											
8											
9											
10											
11											
12											
13											
14											

experience demonstrates that high-risk items contribute more heavily to overall project risk and consequently require heavier weighting.

The following formula is more appropriate because it gives greater weight to the higher severity/probability factor ratings, where the SPR_i are the individual n risk severity/probability factor ratings:

$$\text{Overall Project Risk} = \sqrt{\frac{\sum_{1}^{n}(SPRi)^2}{n}}$$

To illustrate, Table 3-5 represents a project with ten identified risks. A simple average of the risks results in an SPR of 2.10.

The overall project risk formula, with n equal to 10, can be computed as follows. Consistent with intuition and experience, this formula results in a higher severity/probability factor rating than would result from calculating the simple average.

$$\sqrt{\frac{(3^2 \times 4 + 2^2 + 1^2 \times 3)}{10}} = \sqrt{\frac{51}{10}} \approx 2.3$$

Another measure of aggregate project risk is the number of risks at each SPR level. For example, Table 3-5 identifies ten risks for a sample project: four at SPR 3, three at SPR 2, and three at SPR 1. This represents 40 percent of the risks as being high in both severity and probability and another 30 percent as high in at least one risk factor. In other words, the project depicted is potentially very risky.

Additionally, the severity/probability factor ratings can change during a project's lifecycle. By capturing the individual risk SPR change (i.e., SPR Δ), one can calculate the direction of change in aggregate SPR (either by determining the simple average or by using the overall project risk formula). An increasing aggregate SPR would be an early alert that a project is getting into trouble and needs immediate attention to avoid failure.

With all this discussion of numbers and statistics, be careful. Statistics do not manage risk—people and actions do! Although numbers seem to represent objectivity, be careful when relying on mechanistic calculations of overall project risk. The most important approach to dealing with project

TABLE 3-5 Example of Overall Project Risk Calculations

Risk #	1	2	3	4	5	6	7	8	9	10	Simple Average	Overall Project Risk Formula
SPR	3	3	3	3	2	2	2	1	1	1	2.1	2.3

risk is to establish risk mitigation strategies and appropriate contingency plans, and then to manage to them.

ASSUMPTION DEFINITION AND PLANNING TECHNIQUES

As mentioned earlier and in contrast to identifiable risks, unmanaged assumptions are neither visible nor apparent as risks and can be the most dangerous. They are introduced by organizational culture and, when unknowingly present in the project environment, foster incorrect perceptions and unrealistic optimism.

Assumptions are a given in any project. Every project management class and methodology tells us to document our assumptions and to have them verified by the customer or other sources. But do projects manage their assumptions? Typically, when an assumption proves incorrect or a change in environment negates it, reactionary or "cry wolf" behaviors tend to dominate.

Is this the best you can do? No! You must manage assumptions in much the same way as risks; in fact, they are a new source of risk. To avoid surprise, document assumptions about the project and monitor them to ensure that changing circumstances do not negate assumptions and transform them into risks. For every assumption defined and documented, define a metric to test its continued accuracy. By establishing measures for your assumptions and

---

Failed Assumption Example

A state agency was acquiring a document imaging system to help modernize and automate their accounts payable process. Their basic assumption was that the integration vendor could easily provide them with an application design and implementation to optimize their business process. Unfortunately, this was not the case, and the project timeframe began to lengthen as the vendor was forced to provide several iterative designs. Although recognized in time so that the project succeeded, much time was wasted and sponsor anxiety generated before corrective action was taken.

What could have been done to avoid this situation? During the corrective action, it was recognized that an objective measure of the integration vendor's progress would have surfaced the problem much earlier. For example, if a time or iteration limit had been contractually specified, then corrective action would have been triggered earlier. The following possible corrective actions were discussed by the project team:

- Identify and contract with an experienced accounts payable document imaging consultant.
- Allow for more design iterations in the project plan, as this was a pilot project.
- Differentiate between minimal system and process requirements and nice-to-have features.

---

monitoring them, you can ensure that proactively developed contingency plans can be triggered when situations change.

By examining the underlying assumption, defining an appropriate metric, and outlining corrective actions, you can proceed with the project without the stress of not recognizing that assumptions are risks and must be managed.

Assumption Identification Techniques

Project assumptions are derived from three sources:
- Prior project management exposure
- Brainstorming
- Identified risks that have both a low severity and low probability.

Experience-Based Assumptions

Just as prior project experience gives the project manager a source for identifying risk and planning, it provides knowledge about assumptions that hold true within an organization and through various types of projects. For example, experience may show that any new technology implementation effort should have a cost contingency factor of 25 percent, or that sponsor availability can rapidly change during the course of a project. Appropriately documented, these are reasonable assumptions. They must be monitored, however, and tracked for continued justification.

Brainstorming-Based Assumptions

Using the same brainstorming technique described for identifying risk, you can identify assumptions, define a metric to monitor continued applicability, and examine potential mitigation strategies. Table 3-6 provides an example of a few typical assumptions, with possible monitoring metric and mitigation strategies.

Converting Low Risks into Assumptions

The risk mitigation strategy and contingency plan evaluation and planning activity emphasize that a monitoring metric must be established for low-probability and low-severity risks. Once this is done, these risks can be reclassified as assumptions and tracked accordingly.

Assumption Evaluation

Having documented assumptions and identified a monitoring metric and potential mitigation strategy, the project manager and accountable person must periodically test the metric and ensure that no environmental

TABLE 3-6	Example of Assumption Identification and Analysis		
Assumption	**Monitoring Metric**	**Mitigation Strategy**	
Project scope is fixed by requirements definition in the project charter	• Project change requests will alter defined budget, resource, or schedule by less than 5%	• Reject additional change requests • Renegotiate budget, resources. and schedule	
Project team has sufficient experience in business area	• Milestone deliverables are produced on schedule and meet quality metrics	• Provide additional staff training • Provide mentoring	
Project sponsor is readily available for issue/change request resolution	• Issue/change requests are resolved within two days	• Delay project • Reaffirm sponsor availability via Executive Sponsor or Steering Committee • Change issue/change resolution accountability	

change has occurred. If circumstances transform an assumption into a risk, the established risk management process should be invoked.

Figure 3-4 represents a possible format for documenting assumptions and their monitoring measure, potential mitigation strategy, and potential conversion to actual project risks.

ENTERPRISE/PROGRAM RISK MANAGEMENT

In addition to establishing project risk management, consider establishing an enterprise-wide or program-level risk management process. It is common for several major development projects to be occurring simultaneously throughout an organization. Moreover, these projects often encounter similar risks. Evaluating project risks as previously described, it becomes a simple, mechanical process to summarize them and examine the organizational implications of risk over all projects.

If multiple projects identify similar high risks (i.e., SPR of 2 or 3), then their potential impact on the organization as a whole is very high, even if inter-project dependencies are low. Correspondingly, multiple medium project risks (i.e., SPR of 1), while not necessarily of the highest concern to an individual project, represent a greater aggregate risk to the organization.

For example, if multiple projects are simultaneously introducing similar new technologies to the organization, then each project may rate the risk as either high or medium, depending on its project team's skill set and risk aversion mindset. Customers may see or believe only medium-to-low risk, if any, because the vendor marketplace has successfully exaggerated the simplicity of the new technology. It is certainly easy to envision (as well as demonstrate by past experience) that many or most of these new technology efforts will encounter difficulty, and project leaders will be forced to execute risk mitigation strategies and contingency plans.

Examining individual project risks with their mitigation strategies from an enterprise-wide perspective would certainly give a clearer perspective. In addition, the organization can then act as a unit. For example, a pilot project that evaluates the new technology to establish its limits and usefulness might be advisable and should be executed before any dependent project proceeds. This would certainly take advantage of lessons learned and avoid the costly impact of individual project risk mitigation and potential failure.

Successful project risk management will add greatly to the probability of project success. Identifying project risks and assumptions, documenting them, and including them in the overall project plan and processes are not only justifiable activities but necessary ones. At project closure, integrate the project risk and assumption experience into the organization's project management knowledge repository. In future projects, this knowledgebase can serve as the starting point for identifying and analyzing risk. New and experienced project managers can use these past real-world experiences to reduce their worry and burden and to increase their likelihood of success.

CHAPTER 4

Execution: Project Risk Audit

It is a test of true theories not only to account for but to predict phenomena.
—WILLIAM WHEWELL

During the project execution phase, best practices dictate that project deliverables be examined to ensure that they meet the project objectives established during the planning phase. Likewise, management processes should be audited periodically to ensure that they are operating properly. Even the most meticulously planned and managed project can get into difficulty, as every project is an amalgamation of people, processes, and plans in an ever-changing environment. Therefore, monitoring and ensuring the temporal health of a project are critical to its success. Figure 4-1 shows the placement of the project risk audit process within the project management process defined by the *PMBOK® Guide.*

Project managers are familiar with the need to establish plans for measuring deliverable quality. Deliverable quality nevertheless often suffers because project management processes are not in place or are not functioning properly. A project risk audit examines these processes and, through findings and recommendations, gives the project manager methods to ensure that project management processes do not impede success. Project risk auditing should therefore be part of the quality plan for a project.

This chapter outlines a proven, effective technique for conducting a project risk audit. To be most effective, audits must be objective. Accordingly, the audit is best performed by an outside third party with no personal stake in the outcome. If this is not possible, the technique can be applied to a self-audit.

FIGURE 4-1   Execution Process and Risk Audit

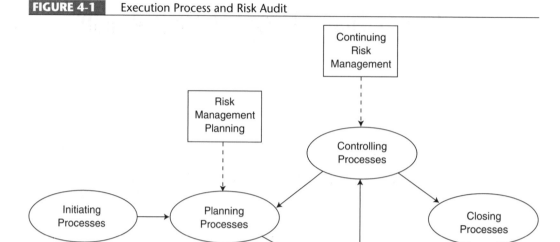

Development of the Project Risk Audit Technique

The risk audit technique outlined in this chapter follows the precepts of project management outlined in the PMI *PMBOK® Guide*. In addition, they take into consideration the key process areas forming the centerpiece of the Software Engineering Institute's Capability Maturity Model for Software (CMM®) Level 2 and 3 organizations. This specific technique was initially developed for the State of Washington's Year 2000 Risk Assessment Program and used to assess state agency and university Year 2000 information technology mitigation efforts. Several private consulting firms (Sterling Associates, Cotey Computer Services, CASE Associates, Management Technology Group, and CIBER) worked with the state's Department of Information Services to develop program and project risk assessment criteria and processes.

The author modified and extended the technique to conduct general project risk audits for non-Y2K projects and programs in the public and private sectors. The technique has proven successful for both information technology and construction projects and is easily adaptable to any project environment. While some risk audit questions are specific to software development projects, you can easily modify them for other project types.

EXECUTING A PROJECT RISK AUDIT

Whether performed internally or as part of an independent validation and verification process, project risk audits should be conducted as objectively and professionally as possible. The purpose is not to condemn the project team or management but to identify and mitigate risk. The emphasis is on project improvement. It is to everyone's advantage to conclude a project successfully—on time, within budget, and satisfying stakeholder requirements. Before beginning the audit, a clear statement by the risk audit sponsor is required to ensure both cooperation and accurate information from the project team and other stakeholders.

Participants

A project risk audit involves everyone associated with the project. It is necessary, but not sufficient, to discuss the project with the project manager. Certainly, the project manager is a central figure, but input from the entire project team, and especially stakeholders, is critical. Table 4-1 summarizes the project risk audit participants.

To be objective, the project risk auditor must be impartial, that is, he or she should have no stake in the outcome of the project. Credibility is also necessary, as audit findings from a non-trusted source can severely damage the morale of the project team and cast unwarranted doubt on the outcome of the project. In large organizations, members of a program/project management office could perform this role, but only if it has organizational

TABLE 4-1 Project Risk Audit Participants

Participant	Involvement
Project Risk Audit Sponsor	• Establishes the scope of the project risk audit • Ensures cooperation from project team and stakeholders
Auditor	• Plans and conducts the project risk audit • Conducts interviews • Analyzes evidence • Prepares findings and recommendations • Presents final audit report
Project Manager	• Coordinates access to project team and stakeholders • Participates in interviews • Presents evidence
Project Team (including external vendors or subcontractors)	• Participates in interview process • Presents evidence
Sponsor	• Participates in interview process
Stakeholders	• Participates in interview process

credibility and support. If the audit needs to meet best practice audit standards, then external risk management consultants should be retained.

Conduct a project risk audit as a mini-project. Doing so requires following the same rigor and formality necessary for any project. With the stakeholders, define and approve a risk audit charter—perhaps a standard one. It should:

- Identify the risk audit sponsor and other stakeholders
- Specify the risk audit's scope and objectives
- Name the participants, along with their roles and responsibilities
- Outline the risk audit plan and schedule.

The audit process examines project management processes and the status of a project through ten critical success factors (CSFs). These are discussed in detail below.

Timetable

An initial project risk audit requires approximately 20 to 70 hours of effort spread over a one- to four-week period. Follow-up risk audits require a shorter period because there is an established baseline and because the focus is on open recommendations to mitigate risks discovered in the prior risk audit. A typical task list and timetable are presented in Table 4-2, and a network diagram of these tasks is shown in Figure 4-2.

The variance in effort and elapsed time is dependent on several factors:

- The level of required documentation
- The organization of existing project documentation
- The availability of project team and sponsor personnel for interviews.

TABLE 4-2 Project Risk Audit Timetable

Task	Effort in Hours	Elapsed Time in Days
Identify interviewees (project sponsor, significant stakeholders, and project members)	1 – 3	½ – 2
Schedule risk audit interviews	1 – 3	½ – 2
Gather risk audit evidence	4 – 8	½ – 2
Conduct risk audit interviews	2 – 8	½ – 4
Analyze project documentation & interview notes	4 – 16	1 – 3
Prepare findings	4 – 16	1 – 3
Prepare recommendations for project risk mitigation	2 – 8	½ – 2
Prepare risk audit report for presentation	2 – 8	½ – 2
Total	20 – 70 hours	5 – 20 days

FIGURE 4-2   Project Risk Audit Process Steps

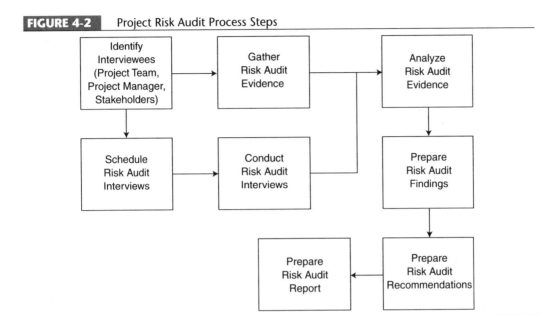

Additionally, the high end of effort and elapsed time estimates are standard if the risk audit findings need to pass generally accepted audit practices.

Risk audits should be included as part of the project plan. Project sponsors will not hesitate to fund periodic audits if the project's quality plan includes them.

Steps

As shown in Table 4-2 and Figure 4-2, the project risk auditor conducts eight major activities in a project risk audit:

1. **Identifying interviewees**—This is the risk auditor's first task. Working in conjunction with the project manager, the auditor identifies two to four individuals who can best describe how the project is proceeding. The project sponsor is the person who will judge the overall success of the project. The risk auditor also looks for other influential stakeholders and senior members of the project team.

2. **Scheduling interviews**—Schedule interviews as soon as possible. Each interview should last approximately one-half to one hour.

3. **Conducting risk audit interviews**—Use the audit working papers (see Figure 4-3) as both a source of interview questions and for recording the results. Because your interview notes are the source of referenced evidence, ensure that the interviewee is comfortable with

FIGURE 4-3   Extract of Risk Audit Working Papers

Project Risk Audit Instrument			
Enterprise:	**Project:**		
Critical Success Factor/Sub-Factor	**Findings / Recommendations**	**Rating**	**Evidence References**
1. The project is appropriately organized.			
1.1 Is the project steering committee comprised of executive decision-makers functioning?	*Finding:*		
	Recommendation:		
1.2 Has an executive sponsor from the business community been designated?	*Finding:*		
	Recommendation:		
1.3 Have project management roles and responsibilities, with lines of authority and accountability, been defined and agreed upon?	*Finding:*		
	Recommendation:		

what you record. You should either read back your notes or provide the interviewee with a copy before issuing the risk audit report. Please note that interview evidence is "soft" evidence and is not sufficient to support a low-risk rating.

4. **Gathering risk audit evidence**—Obtain supporting evidence from the project's documentation. Each CSF question on the risk audit instrument (see Tables 4-5 through 4-14) specifies the type of documentary evidence needed to adequately demonstrate low risk. Typical evidence includes project plans and schedules, status reports and meeting minutes, staffing analysis and budget variance reporting, and test results and defect reports.

5. **Analyzing risk audit evidence**—Analyze the results of the interviews and the content of the collected evidence to determine what risk levels are appropriate for the project. (See the Project Risk Audit Evaluation section below for a description of the risk rating assessment process.)

6. **Preparing risk audit findings**—Document your findings and the associated evidentiary reference (interview and "hard" evidence).

7. **Preparing risk audit recommendations**—Prepare a recommendation to reduce risk for each major and subordinate CSF rated as

medium or high risk. Some organizations may request a "findings only" audit; if so, the risk auditor should perform this. However, the project management experience required to conduct successful audits places the project risk auditor in an excellent position to make project management process improvement recommendations.

8. **Preparing the risk audit report**—Prepare the final risk audit report and deliver it to the risk audit sponsor. In addition, the project manager should receive a copy because he or she will be responsible for responding to the audit and implementing the recommendations.

Project Risk Audit and the "Small" Project

Even if a project is "small," a properly risk-averse and professional project manager will address the management processes outlined in the ten critical success factors. For project manager self-assessment or sponsor-requested review, address the following critical success factors:

- Risk Management (CSF # 2)
    2.4 Is an ongoing risk identification, assessment, and management process in place and operating effectively?
    2.5 Have project assumptions been verified and appropriate monitoring measures put in place to ensure that failed assumptions do not become risks?
- Planning (CSF # 3)
    3.2 Are dependencies among tasks identified, including decision dependencies?
    3.3 Has a schedule been established that is reasonable based on resources (budget), productivity assumptions, and dependencies?
    3.5 Is the project plan used to track progress and updated on a regular basis?
    3.8 Has the project plan been reviewed, approved, and signed off by the project stakeholders?
- Milestones (CSF # 4) – Sub-CSFs 4.2 and 4.3
    4.2 Are major project milestones being met so far?
    4.3 Is there sufficient time (with appropriate slack) to complete the project before the committed completion date?
- Monitoring and Control – Sub-CSFs 5.2 and 5.3
    5.2 Are project status and activities being monitored and reported in enough detail and with enough frequency to ensure early detection of problems or schedule slippage?
    5.3 Is the project budget being appropriately tracked and reported?
- Resources (CSF # 7) – Sub-CSFs 7.2 and 7.5
    7.2 Is the level of effort estimated for each work package at an appropriate activity level, and is it reasonable?
    7.5 Does the project have a sufficient budget to conduct required activities?

By addressing the questions from these four CSFs, "small" project health can be quickly estimated. However, if this estimation points to high risk, then a full project risk audit with formal findings and recommendations may be advisable to minimize risk.

Deliverables

The risk audit working papers (see Figure 4-3) are a major deliverable from the project risk audit process. However, take great caution in their distribution. The working papers reference both interview and documentary evidence. In sensitive political environments, interview evidence may need to remain confidential. During the planning process for a project risk audit, ensure that working paper distribution and confidentiality agreements are established and then followed. The auditor's ability to discern risk-based information often rests on his or her confidentiality credibility with the interviewee. If an interviewee feels threatened by exposure, that person may not be forthcoming, which will likely lead to "covered up" risks.

In addition to the risk audit working papers, a number of other supporting documents are produced during the risk audit process:

- **Interview log**—Contains the interview control number for reference in risk audit working papers, interview date, interviewee name and title, and interviewer name
- **Documentation log**—Contains the document control number for reference in risk audit working papers, a brief description of the document content, the reviewer's name, and the date of the review
- **Audit summary**—Summarizes the findings, assessment rating, and recommendations for the ten CSFs of the sub–CSF-level audit content.

In traditional audit scenarios, the auditor presents only findings. This is definitely at the discretion of the audit sponsor. However, one of the essential characteristics of project risk auditors is their experience in successfully completing projects. You should therefore encourage the audit sponsor to allow recommendations for improvement and risk reduction.

PROJECT RISK AUDIT EVALUATION

Central to the project risk audit process is a set of ten CSFs used to evaluate the effectiveness (i.e., riskiness) of management, planning, resourcing, and other processes essential to a project's success. The ten critical success factors are:

1. **Organization**—The project is appropriately organized.
2. **Risk management**—Project risks are identified and appropriately managed.
3. **Planning**—The project is appropriately planned.
4. **Milestones**—Project milestones are being met on schedule.

5. **Monitoring and control**—The project status is appropriately monitored and adequately controlled.
6. **Scope change control**—The project scope is appropriately controlled.
7. **Resources**—The project has the appropriate resources.
8. **Functional testing**—Appropriate functional acceptance testing processes and plans are in place.
9. **Capacity and performance testing**—Appropriate capacity and performance acceptance testing processes and plans are in place.
10. **Training**—Appropriate and timely training is available.

Each critical success factor divides into sub-CSFs, which provide detailed evaluation questions and assessment criteria. Depending on the project type and environment, the sub-factors defining each critical success factor may require modification or extension. Assign assessment ratings using a simple three-level system: high, medium, and low risk. Apply the following rating definitions for the assessment:

- **High**—Evaluation criteria and documentation are not addressed, are missing, or are substantially incomplete.
- **Medium**—Evaluation criteria and documentation are substantially complete but require more detail.
- **Low**—Evaluation criteria and acceptable documentation are completely addressed.

Document the findings for the sub-CSFs with appropriate references to supporting interview notes or other documentation (i.e., "cataloged evidence"). After analyzing the sub-CSFs, assign an overall assessment rating. To provide a moderately conservative risk audit, use the following guidelines (detailed in Table 4-3) for each major critical success factor rating:

- If one-third or more of the sub-CSFs are high risk, rate the CSF as high risk.
- If half or more of the sub-CSFs are low risk and there are no high risk ratings, assign the CSF a low-risk rating.
- Rate any other combination as medium risk.

In extreme situations in which project process failure would have disastrous results, a more conservative approach for rating evaluation is justifiable. That is, if at least one sub-CSF assesses as high risk, then the CSF is high risk. If at least one sub-CSF assesses as medium risk with no high-risk sub-CSFs, then the CSF is medium risk. Finally, the CSF may be assessed as low risk if and only if *all* sub-CSFs are low risk.

TABLE 4-3 Individual Project Risk Audit CSF Rating Evaluation

		Critical Success Factor Rating		
Critical Success Factor	# Sub-CSFs	Low	Medium	High
Organization	3	0 High & ≥ 2 Low	≤ 1 Low & 0 High	≥ 1 High
Risk Management	5	0 High & ≥ 3 Low	1 High or < 3 Low	≥ 2 High
Planning	8	0 High & ≥ 4 Low	1 High or < 4 Low	≥ 2 High
Milestones	3	0 High & ≥ 2 Low	≤ 1 Low & 0 High	≥ 1 High
Monitoring & Control	4	0 High & ≥ 2 Low	1 High or < 2 Low	≥ 1 High
Scope Change Control	3	0 High & ≥ 2 Low	≤ 1 Low & 0 High	≥ 1 High
Resources	5	0 High & ≥ 3 Low	1 High or < 3 Low	≥ 2 High
Functional Testing	5	0 High & ≥ 3 Low	1 High or < 3 Low	≥ 2 High
Capacity & Performance Testing	6	0 High & ≥ 3 Low	1 High or < 3 Low	≥ 2 High
Training	4	0 High & ≥ 2 Low	≤ 1 Low & 0 High	≥ 1 High

As well as establishing a rating for the major critical success factors, create a recommendation for action to reduce risk for each high- or medium-risk sub-CSF. Use a similar strategy to rate the overall project risk (see Table 4-4). If four or more CSFs assess as high risk, the overall rating is high. If six or more ratings are low and there are no high ratings, the overall rating is low. Any other combination rates as medium risk. In the final risk audit report presented to the stakeholder, recommendations for high and medium risks are proposed as actions that should be taken to reduce the risk audit rating to low.

This technique requires little training and no project-specific knowledge. A typical initial risk audit can be completed in 20 to 70 hours of effort, depending on the availability of necessary interviewees, the state of project documentation, and the required level of reference documentation and supporting evidence. Follow-up risk audits require less time because open recommendations on high and medium critical success factors become the focus of evaluation.

TABLE 4-4 Overall CSF Rating

Individual CSF Ratings			
Low	Medium	High	Overall Rating
≥ 6	—	0	Low
—	≥ 5	≤3	Medium
—	—	≥ 4	High
—	Number Irrelevant		

If a program of multiple projects is the scope of the risk audit, it is appropriate to establish an audit oversight function to review each audit. The oversight function will ensure that:

- Appropriate due diligence is applied to each audit
- The same risk audit standards are followed
- Appropriate evidence supports findings and ratings
- Audit results are credible.

In many organizations, this could fall within the scope of a project or program management office.

This technique concentrates on the "correctness" of the risk audit rather than on a numerical rating system. The findings and recommendations form the core of the technique. That is, while it is important to identify the risk level and even boldly display it in color on presentations (e.g., high = red, medium = yellow, and low = green), the principal value is in the recommended corrective actions to reduce risk and better ensure success.

As stated, provide supporting evidence for the findings—specifically, interview notes and actual documentation. It is essential to be objective when evaluating evidence. Just as in a financial audit, the feelings and impressions of the auditor are not important. Findings represent a summary gathered from referenced evidence. Document evidence references in the audit working papers (see Figure 4-3).

PROJECT RISK AUDIT CRITICAL SUCCESS FACTORS

Following is a description of each of the CSFs and their sub-CSF evaluation questions. Tables 4-5 through 4-14 detail the evaluation questions and

TABLE 4-5 Organization Critical Success Factor (CSF #1)

CSF	Factor	Criteria/Acceptable Documentation
1.	**The project is appropriately organized.**	
1.1	Is a project steering committee comprised of executive decision makers functioning?	• Project organization chart • Project charter • Meeting minutes
1.2	Has an executive sponsor from the business community been designated?	• Project organization chart • Project charter • Meeting minutes
1.3	Have project management roles and responsibilities, with lines of authority and accountability, been defined, assigned, and agreed upon?	• Resource assignment matrix • Project organization chart • Project charter • Meeting minutes

TABLE 4-6 Risk Management Critical Success Factor (CSF #2)

CSF	Factor	Criteria/Acceptable Documentation
2.	**Project risks are identified and appropriately managed.**	
2.1	Have project risks been identified and categorized as to likelihood and impact?	Risks are documented and categorized as to likelihood and impact.
2.2	Are appropriate risk mitigation strategies in place with appropriate monitoring measures?	• Risk mitigation strategies have been developed, documented, and implemented. • Applicable metrics are in place to monitor effectiveness of mitigation strategy.
2.3	For high-probability or high-impact risks, have contingency plans been developed in case the risk mitigation strategy fails?	• Contingency plans have been developed and documented for high-probability and high-impact risks in case a risk mitigation strategy fails. • Appropriate metrics are monitored to determine when or why to trigger implementation of the contingency plan.
2.4	Is an ongoing risk identification, assessment, and management process in place and operating effectively?	• Meeting minutes • Status reports
2.5	Have project assumptions been verified and appropriate monitoring measures been put in place to ensure that failed assumptions do not become risks?	• Project assumptions are documented. • Appropriate metrics are established to monitor continued validity of assumptions.

evaluation criteria or acceptable documentation for verification of completeness for each CSF.

Organization (CSF # 1)

This factor assesses the breadth and depth of the project's organization and the commitment to the project within the organization to determine if the project's organizational structure can manage both tactical and strategic project issues. Projects without proper sponsorship and management oversight will incur many problems, especially in issue and change request resolution. In addition, lack of explicitly defined project roles and responsibilities will create confusion and decidedly affect all decision-making processes. Examine documented project organization charts, roles and responsibility matrices, project charter definitions, and minutes from project and sponsor meetings for supporting evidence for this CSF.

Risk Management (CSF # 2)

This CSF assesses the risk identification, mitigation strategy, and contingency planning for high-probability or high-impact risks. It also assesses

TABLE 4-7 Planning Critical Success Factor (CSF #3)

CSF	Factor	Criteria/Acceptable Documentation
3.	**The project is appropriately planned.**	
3.1	Are all appropriate tasks identified in the work breakdown structure (WBS) or project plan?	Major task categories *may* include: • Project management • Requirements analysis, design, and documentation • Construction and testing of deliverables • Preparing test environment • Testing (functionality and capacity/performance) • Interface testing • Implementation
3.2	Are dependencies among tasks identified, including decision dependencies?	• Critical path chart or network diagram • List of dependencies
3.3	Has a schedule been established, and is it reasonable based on resources (budget), productivity assumptions, and dependencies?	• Gantt chart • Schedule • Timeline • Calendar
3.4	Is the plan clear and detailed enough to monitor progress?	Documentation in enough detail that would allow the project manager to know project progress at all times and when the schedule may be affected
3.5	Is the project plan used to track progress and updated on a regular basis?	• Updated project plans • Status reports that track actual against planned
3.6	Are external project dependencies identified in the plan?	• Critical path chart • List of dependencies
3.7	Have appropriate interim and major milestones been defined?	Identified interim and major milestones
3.8	Has the project plan been reviewed, approved, and signed off by the project stakeholders?	Approved project plan

the continuing validity of high-impact assumptions. Proactive risk mitigation is key to a project's likelihood of success. Examine the project's risk management plan for supporting documentation.

Planning (CSF # 3)

This CSF provides an assessment of the breadth and depth of project planning, scope definition, scheduling, and identification of external dependencies. An appropriately detailed and managed plan is an absolute requirement for successful project management; therefore, scrutinize the plan closely. Although supporting evidence is most easily assessed using a project management planning and tracking tool (e.g., MS Project, Primavera, Scitor

PS7), such a tool is not required. Assessment of the Planning CSF examines the components of a plan—not how they are documented or accomplished.

TABLE 4-8 Milestones Critical Success Factor (CSF #4)

CSF	Factor	Criteria/Acceptable Documentation
4.	**Project milestones are being met on schedule.**	
4.1	Are interim project milestones being met so far? If NOT: • What were the reasons for the delays? • Are more delays likely? • Are future delays being mitigated and how? • Are delays affecting major milestones?	• Status reports showing interim milestones being accomplished as scheduled • Critical path calculation, revised schedule, issue papers and logs, mitigation strategies
4.2	Are major project milestones being met so far? If NOT: • What were the reasons for the delays? • Are more delays likely? • Is the final completion date affected? • How are future delays being mitigated?	• Status reports showing major milestone completion as scheduled • Critical path calculation, revised schedule, issue papers and logs, mitigation strategies
4.3	Is there sufficient time (with appropriate slack) to complete the project before the committed completion date?	Documentation of project schedule with sufficient slack to accommodate future unforeseen schedule delays

TABLE 4- Monitoring and Control Critical Success Factor (CSF #5)

CSF	Factor	Criteria/Acceptable Documentation
5.	**The project is appropriately monitored and adequately controlled.**	
5.1	Does the project receive appropriate and timely executive and business sponsor attention?	• Status meetings and reports • Evidence of timely decision making
5.2	Are project status and activities being monitored and reported in enough detail and with enough frequency to ensure early detection of problems or schedule slippage?	• Actual hours tracked against estimates • % complete against schedules and estimates • Counts of implementation units completed • Documented project meetings and progress reports • Schedule variance • Schedule performance index from earned value calculations
5.3	Is the project budget being appropriately tracked and reported?	• Spreadsheets with budget information • Budget status reports to sponsors • Budget actuals tracked against estimates • Actuals compared to % complete • Cost variance • Cost performance index from earned value calculations
5.4	Are external project dependencies included in status reporting?	• Status meetings and reports • Documented project meetings and progress reports

TABLE 4-10 Scope Change Control Critical Success Factor (CSF #6)

CSF	Factor	Criteria/Acceptable Documentation
6.	**The project scope is appropriately controlled.**	
6.1	Are issues appropriately identified, escalated, and resolved in a timely manner?	• Issue log • Meeting minutes • Status reports • Change requests • Change impact analysis
6.2	Are change requests effectively recognized, analyzed for impact, and approved prior to inclusion in the project scope?	• Change control log • Approved change requests • Revised project plan baseline to reflect approved changes
6.3	Are appropriate configuration management practices in place and being followed?	• Configuration management policy and procedures • Evidence of versioning in practice • Configuration status accounting

TABLE 4-11 Resources Critical Success Factor (CSF #7)

CSF	Factor	Criteria/Acceptable Documentation
7.	**The project is appropriately resourced.**	
7.1	Is the level of effort estimated for each work package at an appropriate activity level, and is it reasonable?	• Resource leveling in project software • Spreadsheet of hour allocation with daily or weekly totals for each resource • Evidence of contingency for "discoveries"
7.2	Are appropriate staff resources (skill set and quantity) available and assigned to complete project implementation?	• Evidence that appropriate skills and knowledge are assigned to specific work packages • Business staff and operations staff are involved where necessary • External resource assignments
7.3	Are appropriate staff support resources (skill set and quantity) available and assigned to provide ongoing maintenance and enhancement?	• Evidence that appropriate skills and knowledge are assigned to specific work packages • Business staff and operations staff involved where necessary • External resource assignments
7.4	Are appropriate tools and other necessary facilities available and effectively utilized?	• Documented capacity estimates, tool requirements, and identification • Actual use of tools • Appropriate manual process where tools are not available or appropriate • Appropriate supporting facilities are available
7.5	Does the project have a sufficient budget to conduct required activities?	• Budget document based on reasonable estimates resulting from a thorough assessment and appropriate activities

TABLE 4-12 Functional Testing Critical Success Factor (CSF #8)

CSF	Factor	Criteria/Acceptable Documentation
8.	**Appropriate functional acceptance-testing processes and plans are in place.**	
8.1	Do the currently contracted functional specifications match the current operational needs?	Documentation attesting to functional specification match or non-match
8.2	Are the owning business users and management involved in establishing the functional acceptance testing scope and standards?	• Meeting minutes • Interviews
8.3	Are functional acceptance test processes appropriate, and are results monitored and tracked?	• Test plans • Test scripts • Involvement of business staff to ensure that appropriate business rules are being tested • Acceptance criteria • Confirmation of results tracking the completion of tests at various stages • Independent tests or verification results • Tracking of fixes and re-tests
8.4	Are functional system interface test plans developed, followed, and tracked?	• Test plans • Test scripts • Involvement of business staff to ensure appropriate business rules are being tested • Acceptance criteria • Confirmation of results tracking the completion of tests at various stages • Independent tests or verification results • Tracking of fixes and re-tests
8.5	Is comprehensive end-to-end functional acceptance testing performed or planned, including testing of all software, hardware, and telecommunications components?	• Test plans • Test results

Milestones (CSF # 4)

This CSF assesses the scheduled completion of interim and major project milestones and their impact on overall project completion. Milestone completion is a true measure of progress and a credible predictor of the future.

Beware of measuring project progress simply by task and activity completion. While important, individual task completion often represents little "earned value." Milestones established during project planning represent concrete measures of progress from the stakeholders' point of view. For example, on a software development project, completion of individual modules is not as relevant as an implemented subsystem. Likewise, on a construction project, laying two million bricks on time is significant to

TABLE 4-13 Capacity and Performance Testing Critical Success Factor (CSF #9)

CSF	Factor	Criteria/Acceptable Documentation
9.	**Appropriate capacity and performance acceptance-testing processes and plans are in place.**	
9.1	Do the currently contracted capacity and performance specifications match the current operational needs? *If YES:* • What forecasting methodology was used to determine the contracted and current operational needs? • Is this a "best practice" forecasting methodology?	Documentation attesting to capacity and performance specification match or non-match
9.2	Are the owning business users and management involved in establishing the capacity and performance acceptance testing scope and standards?	• Meeting minutes • Interviews
9.3	Are capacity and performance acceptance test processes appropriate, and are results monitored and tracked?	• Test plans • Test scripts • Involvement of business staff to ensure that appropriate business rules are being tested • Acceptance criteria • Confirmation of results tracking the completion of tests at various stages • Independent tests or verification results • Tracking of fixes and re-tests.
9.4	Are capacity and performance system interface test plans developed, followed, and tracked?	• Test plans • Test scripts • Involvement of business staff to ensure that appropriate business rules are being tested • Acceptance criteria • Confirmation of results tracking the completion of tests at various stages • Independent tests or verification results • Tracking of fixes and re-tests
9.5	Is comprehensive end-to-end capacity and performance acceptance testing performed or planned, including testing of all software, hardware, and telecommunications components?	• Test plans • Test results
9.6	Are infrastructure conditions (down to the computing hardware level) that may affect the application being considered, tested, and resolved?	• Inventory of infrastructure dependencies • End-to-end tests of system • Other documents

the subcontractor but may not represent progress to the builder unless the structure is operational. The point is that the project plan should define milestones that measure progress from the stakeholders' perspective.

TABLE 4-14 Training Critical Success Factor (CSF #10)

CSF	Factor	Criteria/Acceptable Documentation
10.	**Appropriate and timely training is available.**	
10.1	Are appropriate training materials available for administration and support staff?	• Training materials • Review of training materials by administrative and support staff as to sufficiency
10.2	Are administration and support staff training appropriately planned and scheduled?	• Training plans • Training schedules • Training part of project master plan
10.3	Are appropriate training materials available for system users?	• Training materials • Review of training materials by system users as to sufficiency
10.4	Is system user training appropriately planned and scheduled?	• Training plans • Training schedules

Monitoring and Control (CSF # 5)

Assessment of this CSF examines the project status reporting process for task completion and budgeting. Only through appropriate monitoring and control can the project manager and sponsor expect to comprehend status, address project slippage, and take corrective action.

Scope Change Control (CSF # 6)

Scope change control assesses the implementation and adherence to issue, change request, and configuration management processes. Ineffective scope change control is one of the important reasons that projects are late and over budget.

Resources (CSF # 7)

This CSF assesses three resource components:
• The capacity and skill set of the assigned project staff (development and maintenance)
• Supporting tools and facilities
• Budget or financial resources.

The availability of required resources forms the justification basis for project plans; if resources are not available when the project is scheduled, the likelihood of failure is high unless treated as a risk and mitigated.

Functional Testing (CSF # 8)

The Functional Testing CSF provides an assessment of the functional capabilities of the system against current operational needs. Incomplete functional testing will be extremely detrimental to successful implementation. As operational and environmental requirements can change during the life of a project, it is mandatory that the owning business users and their management participate in functional testing. While scope changes may arise because of changing requirements, only complete functional testing ensures mapping function to requirements.

Capacity and Performance Testing (CSF # 9)

This factor provides an assessment of the capacity and performance capabilities of the system against operational needs. Even if functionality addresses requirements, implementation will likely be unsuccessful in the eyes of stakeholders if the delivered system cannot sustain real-world loads and expanding scalability requirements. As with functionality, requirement changes in capacity and performance characteristics may cause changes in scope.

Training (CSF # 10)

The Training CSF provides an assessment of the training plans and materials for administrative, support, and user staff. Historically, training has been one of the first deliverables sacrificed when a project encounters difficulties. However, history has also shown that without appropriate training, successful implementation is problematical at best.

Not surprisingly, initial reactions to project risk audits are mixed and often negative. Recriminations, finger pointing, and excuses are common initial reactions to high and medium risk ratings. However, practicality takes over after wounded egos are soothed. Project managers recognize that the risk audit is objective and is not a personal attack or condemnation. By responding to audit recommendations, project managers find that risks are reduced and that they are much more likely to meet their projected completion targets.

Moreover, the reactions of project sponsors are uniformly positive. Although they may not like hearing about potential risks, they are appreciative of the effort because it allows them to take remedial action before it is too late. Using risk audits and openly discussing findings furthers an atmosphere of open communication about risks in the enterprise. In addition, the risk audit process demonstrates to both project sponsors and other stakeholders that they play a critical role in project success. This realization usually leads to increased user involvement and a concomitant positive impact on project progress.

As an added benefit, many enterprises begin to incorporate the content of the ten critical success factors into their project management approach. It may be no surprise that this is usually at the request or demand of stakeholder project sponsors and management rather than the technical project organizations. While by no means a formal project management improvement process as defined by the Software Engineering Institute's Capability Maturity Model, this project risk audit technique can help move an organization in the right direction.

CHAPTER 5

Controlling: Continuing Risk Management

The bitterness of poor quality remains long after the sweetness of meeting the schedule has been forgotten.

—UNATTRIBUTED

A s defined by the Project Management Institute in the *PMBOK® Guide*, continuing risk management is part of the project controlling processes, as pictured in Figure 5-1. Continuous risk management is as important as risk planning. It is one thing to plan for risks that may occur; it is another to ensure that previously identified risks and assumptions do not introduce the possibility of failure.

Figure 5-2 outlines a process for continuing risk management. As shown, there are three basic paths through the process, all ending in the invocation of issue and change management processes to manage the impact of risk.

EXECUTING CONTINUING RISK MANAGEMENT

Continuing risk management is the responsibility of the project manager, with the aid of the project team, customer sponsors, and other customer stakeholders. As shown in Figure 5-2, there are three parallel paths to deal with previously identified risks, previously identified assumptions, and newly identified risks. As with other controlling processes, risk management is continuous throughout project execution.

Participants

While the project manager is ultimately responsible and accountable for continuing risk management, he or she requires the support of the project team members, sponsors, and stakeholders (see Table 5-1).

Timetable

Because continuing risk management is an ongoing task, there is no activity-based timetable to follow. Rather, it is a set of activities to perform

FIGURE 5-1 Controlling Processes and Continuing Risk Management

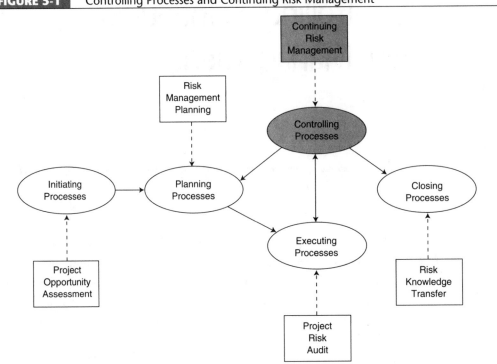

again and again. The project manager may delegate risk and assumption-monitoring activities to various individuals on the project team during the risk management planning process.

Steps

The three parallel paths in the continuing risk management process (as illustrated in Figure 5-2) ensure that the risk management plans developed during the planning phase are executed by continuously monitoring the risk and assumption triggers. The process also accounts for new risk identification.

1. **Monitoring identified risk triggers**—The project manager or other designated individual tracks each identified risk to determine if it has occurred or if the implemented risk mitigation strategy has failed.

    1.1. **Invoking risk management strategy**—If a previously identified risk has occurred (i.e., has been triggered), then it is time to implement the planned risk mitigation strategy. For low-impact

FIGURE 5-2   Continuing Risk Management Process Steps

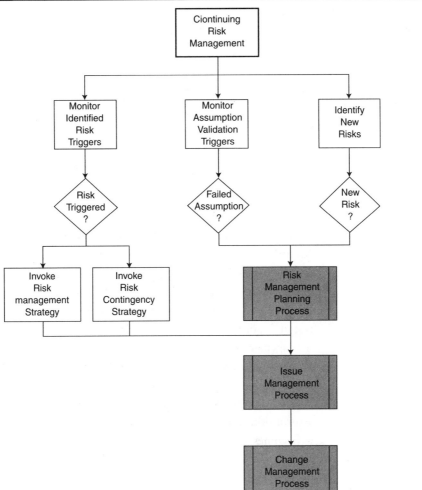

and low-severity risks, this may include detailed planning and budgeting for risk mitigation (see Chapter 3).

1.2. **Invoking risk contingency plan**—If an implemented risk mitigation strategy fails, it is then time to implement the contingency plan. If no contingency plan is available from risk management planning, then detailed planning must occur (see Chapter 3).

2. **Monitoring assumption validation triggers**—The project manager or designated individual continuously checks the assumption validation metric established during risk management planning. If the

TABLE 5-1   Continuing Risk Management Participants

Participant	Involvement
Project Manager	• Coordinates project team, stakeholders, and sponsors • Facilitates risk and assumption trigger monitoring • Leads risk and assumption issue resolution and change management
Project Team (including external vendors or subcontractors)	• Participates in monitoring of risk and assumption triggers • Aids in new risk identification • Participates in risk and assumption issue resolution
Sponsor	• Participates in risk and assumption issue resolution • Participates in risk and assumption change management
Stakeholders	• Participates in risk and assumption issue resolution

assumption becomes invalid, the assumption is now a full-fledged risk, requiring detailed planning (see Chapter 3).

3. **Identifying new risks**—Using the same techniques employed during risk management planning, the project manager, project team, and customer stakeholders continuously examine the project environment for incidents or situations that will affect project deliverable scope, resources, or schedule. If such an incident occurs, the established risk management planning process should be executed.

4. **Executing the risk management planning process**—See Chapter 3 for an explanation of the process.

5. **Executing the issue management process**—Whenever a risk or assumption-monitoring metric is triggered or a new risk is identified, it becomes an issue for the project's established issue management process. This is necessary to ensure that all affected individuals are notified and have input into resolving the issue.

6. **Executing the change management process**—Unless previously established plans, budgets, and resources are available, risk management issue resolution will likely require changes to the project's plan. The project manager must ensure that the agreed-upon change management process handles the impact of issue resolution and approval of changes to project scope, resources, and schedule. Even if a general risk contingency budget is available, approval to allocate the funds requires approval through the change management process.

Deliverables

Continuing risk management creates two deliverables. For the most part, these are merely updates to existing risk management strategies and

Continuing Risk Management and the "Small" Project

If little or no attention was paid to risk identification and response planning during the project's planning phase because it was deemed a "small" project with well-understood scope, deliverables, and effort estimates, then the project can slip into a failure scenario quite easily. Therefore, special attention is required during continuing risk management. That is, the project manager will need to be constantly on guard and consciously examine the project for new risks. Since the reason that risk planning was avoided or minimized was the assumption that scope, deliverables, and work effort are well-understood, then this is where the project manager must concentrate his/her focus.

"Small" projects can often be successfully completed by heroic efforts of the project team, but this is not the way to build long-term team cohesiveness and morale. Keep careful track of changing circumstances and risks that emerge, and be sure that project closure activities document risks that occur and what was done to mitigate them. If failure to do thorough risk identification and mitigation strategy planning had an adverse effect on project outcomes or resource overallocation, learn from the experience and do not repeat it! Sponsors may not agree with thorough risk management processes, but they will penalize failure.

contingency plans. In the case of failed assumptions or newly identified risks, new risk management strategies and contingency plans are developed. In addition, continuous risk management creates input to the issue and change management processes, which in turn create changes to the project's plan.

The two continuing risk management deliverables are:

1. **Risk management report**—As specified by the communications plan developed during the project planning phase, the project manager reports the status of risk management and any impact on the project scope, resources, and schedule. Depending on project complexity, this may be a separate report or may be included as a section of the periodic project status report.

2. **Updated risk management plan**—The project manager ensures that any continuous risk management actions are included in the risk management plan. If these actions require project scope changes, they should be included in a revised project plan baseline as approved by the project's customer sponsor. Even if the risk-based changes are covered by contingency funds and resources, revising the baseline project plan ensures that all project participants are aware of them.

Continuous risk management requires no special techniques or knowledge. The project manager is responsible for ensuring that changing project environmental conditions and other factors do not introduce unmitigated risk. The emphasis for success is on pre-planning. The more thought and time spent in risk management planning (as described in Chapter 3), the more likely that continuing risk management will be both undemanding and successful.

CHAPTER 6

Closure: Risk Knowledge Transfer

*Fools you are. To say you learn by your experience. I prefer to profit by others'
mistakes and avoid the price of my own.*

—Otto Von Bismarck

Du,

D uring the closure phase of a project, it is standard practice to complete a
debriefing of the project team and customer stakeholders and sponsors.
This debriefing provides the basis for an evaluation of the project's success
and lessons learned. These lessons learned allow the continuous improvement of an enterprise's project management processes. Figure 6-1 illustrates
the placement of risk knowledge transfer in the processes defined by the
PMBOK® Guide.

Risk management success or failure is of special importance in this
debriefing and evaluation. As described in the risk management planning
process (see Chapter 3), experience-based risk assessment is a critical element
of the process. While actual experience with risk makes an indelible imprint
on an individual project manager, it is invaluable for other project managers
to gain the value of this knowledge without experiencing the trauma. Figure
6-2 outlines the steps in the process.

EXECUTING RISK KNOWLEDGE TRANSFER

Project management best practices call for a formal project closure phase
to be part of the project plan. Even if a project is an outstanding success and
all involved want to move on to the next project, evaluating what went well
and what can be improved is invaluable. The project manager is responsible
for ensuring the execution of project closure plans.

Participants

Everyone involved with the project participates in the closure debriefing
and evaluation, as outlined in Table 6-1.

FIGURE 6-1   Closure Process and Risk Knowledge Transfer

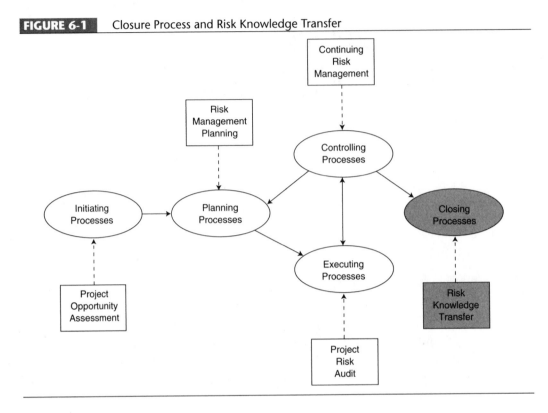

Timetable

The debriefing and evaluation of risk mitigation success or failure is a short-term activity that should begin simultaneously with final project deliverable acceptance. If risk management plans were maintained during

TABLE 6-1   Risk Knowledge Transfer Participants

Participant	Involvement
Project Manager	• Coordinates access to project team, stakeholders, and sponsors • Facilitates risk success/failure debriefing and evaluation • Documents risk success/failure and recommendations for alternative risk mitigation strategies and contingency plans • Archives risk success/failure information
Project Team (including external vendors or subcontractors)	• Provides input on risk mitigation success/failure and recommendations for future improvements
Sponsor	• Provides input on risk mitigation success/failure and recommendations for future improvements
Stakeholders	• Provides input on risk mitigation success/failure and recommendations for future improvements

the project's execution phase, then the process will be brief. It is appropriate to conduct it during the general project evaluation, and it should take only a few hours.

Steps

As illustrated in Figure 6-2, there are four steps in the process of risk knowledge transfer. The focus is to determine the success or failure of risk management planning to provide the basis for future risk identification and mitigation. As noted, the project manager leads the risk knowledge transfer process.

1. **Debriefing project participants**—Three distinct viewpoints are applicable to project evaluation, especially risk: that of the customer sponsor, the customer stakeholders, and the project team. While it is possible to interview all three groups at once, it is preferable to separate them into distinct interview sessions to avoid hesitancy to speak out because of political considerations.

   Just as for any facilitated session, the project manager should prepare a list of questions for the debriefing participants and share them before the debriefing to make the most productive use of time. Some possible questions are:
   - How do you rate the overall effectiveness of the risk management plan? Why?
   - What would you do differently in the future to improve risk mitigation?
   - For any failed risk management strategy, how would you recommend addressing it in the future?
   - For any failed risk contingency plan, how would you recommend addressing it in the future?
   - Should any assumption that later proved invalid be classified as a risk in the future?

   Pay special attention to failed risk mitigation that is within the scope of control of the debriefing participant.

FIGURE 6-2   Risk Knowledge Transfer Process Steps

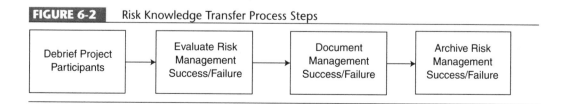

2. **Evaluating risk management success/failure**—Following debriefing interviews with project participants, the project manager will evaluate the observations concerning risk management. This evaluation should include both quantitative and qualitative components.

    Quantitative observations are usually obvious, as they bear directly on variances to the baseline project plan's scope, resources, and schedule. If the project uses a proper change management process, risk mitigation strategy and contingency plans will be reflected in the project plan and can be measured directly.

    Qualitative input from the project participants is important, especially if the project manager anticipates repeat project work with the customer. Customer sponsor and stakeholder perceptions of success or failure help determine the likelihood of further work. Even if circumstances outside the project's control affect its success, customer perception of credible and professional handling of risk is important.

3. **Documenting risk management success/failure**—The project manager should update the risk management planning documents (see Figure 3-3) to reflect the information gathered during the project debriefing sessions. If an automated repository is available, the information should also be reflected there (see Risk Knowledgebase Metadata, below).

4. **Archiving risk management success/failure**—The updated risk management planning documents become part of the permanent project documentation. If an automated enterprise risk repository is available, they should be reflected there as well.

Deliverables

As mentioned, the deliverable from the risk knowledge transfer process is an updated set of documents reflecting the success or failure of the risk

---

Risk Knowledge Transfer and the "Small" Project

If thorough risk management processes were not included in the project's planning and execution phases, then there may seem little point in including risk knowledge transfer in the closure phase. Few projects avoid the impact of risk. If risk plans are not in place, then risk responses are ad hoc and reactive. If this happens, it is most important to document the responses so mistakes can be avoided in the future. If heroic efforts avoided failure, then share this knowledge and avoid repeating the mistake in the future. While a project manager will never forget the failed assumptions leading to reactive risk response, by sharing the knowledge, you can help others avoid having to learn from their own mistakes.

management plan. These must be shared with all project managers and made available for future project risk management planning. The Risk Knowledgebase and Metadata section below outlines one view of an automated risk management repository.

RISK KNOWLEDGEBASE AND METADATA

The most convenient way to store risk experience knowledge and make it accessible is to build an automated repository that resides in a shareable database. Figure 6-3 contains a conceptual entity-relationship (ER) diagram for such a repository. Simply, an entity-relationship diagram represents the things about which we need to know information (entities) and illustrates how they are associated with each other (relationships). While the information modeling community has precise definitions for numerous modeling techniques and their respective diagramming conventions, the following definitions suffice for illustrative purposes:

- A box represents an entity that is information about a person, place, thing, or concept about which we wish to define information. For example, *Customer* and *Project* are entities.
- The lines connecting entities, as shown in the Figure 6-3 ER diagram, represent the relationship between two entities. The numbers at each end of the relationship line determine the cardinality of the relationship; relationships are two-way. For example, a customer sponsors zero or more projects; conversely, a project is sponsored by one and only one customer.

To be useful, a diagram must be meaningful in common language and understandable by business and technical professionals alike. In this vein, Figure 6-3 defines a risk knowledgebase as follows:

1. A customer sponsors zero, one, or more projects. A project is always sponsored by one customer.
2. A project always has one or more risks. A risk is always associated with one project.
3. A risk is classified by one category. A category classifies multiple risks.
4. A risk is assigned one probability. A probability can be assigned to multiple risks.
5. A risk exhibits one severity. A severity can be exhibited by multiple risks.
6. A risk is placed in one timeframe. The same timeframe can be placed on many risks.

FIGURE 6-3   Risk Knowledgebase Entity-Relationship (ER) Diagram

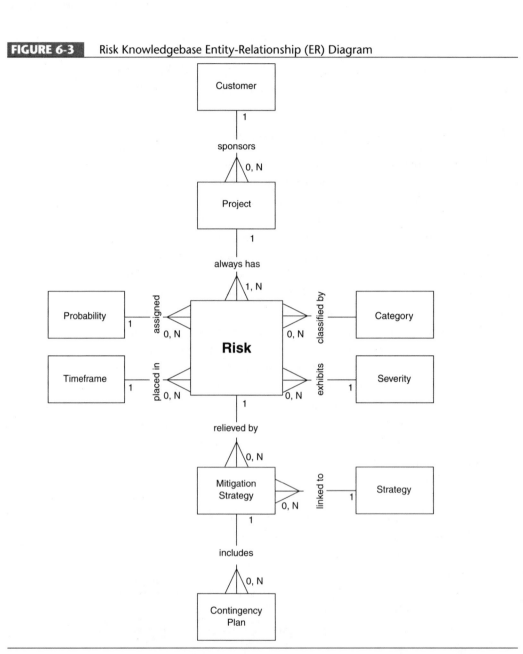

7. A risk is relieved by zero or more mitigation strategies. A mitigation strategy relieves one risk.
8. A risk is linked to a strategy. A strategy can be linked to many risks.
9. A mitigation strategy includes zero or more contingency plans. A contingency plan is included with one mitigation strategy.

Risk Knowledgebase Structure

From the conceptual, logical model of Figure 6-3, and using a database management system such as Microsoft Access, we can construct a physical database repository in which to store the risk knowledgebase. Figure 6-4 shows an example of such a database constructed with MS Access 2000. The attributes for the entities and their implemented database tables are derived from the risk management worksheet defined in Chapter 3 (see Figure 3-3).

Risk Knowledgebase Tables

There are ten basic tables in the sample risk knowledgebase database shown in Figure 6-4. Each enterprise should examine the contents and determine the additional attributes (i.e., database columns) that are required. For example, the Customer table contains only a unique identifier and the customer name; certainly more information is required. The following describes the metadata for each table in the risk knowledge database structure illustrated in Figure 6-4.

FIGURE 6-4   Risk Knowledgebase Database Structure

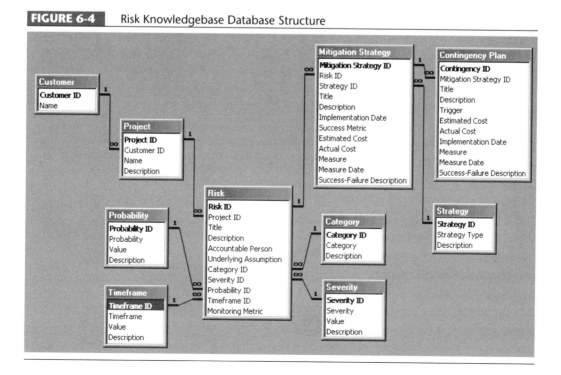

Customer

The Customer table contains necessary information about the project sponsor. For demonstration purposes, Figure 6-5 defines only two attributes.

Project

The Project table contains project definition information. Figure 6-6 defines the table's fields (attributes or columns), data type, and description.

Risk

The Risk table is the core table of the risk knowledgebase repository. It defines the characteristics of the risk and its potential impact on the project. Figure 6-7 contains a definition of the Risk table structure.

Mitigation Strategy

The Mitigation Strategy table contains information about the strategy that the project will use to mitigate a specific risk. While usually only one mitigation strategy is defined for a risk, it may be prudent to define multiple strategies depending on the severity, probability, and timeframe. Figure 6-8 illustrates the structure of the Mitigation Strategy table.

Contingency Plan

For risks that have high severity and probability, it is important to define a risk contingency plan to take effect if the mitigation strategy fails. Figure 6-9 outlines the contents of such a table.

FIGURE 6-5   Customer Table

Customer : Table

Field Name	Data Type	Description
Customer ID	AutoNumber	DBMS assigned ID for Customer
Name	Text	Name of Customer

FIGURE 6-6   Project Table

Project : Table

Field Name	Data Type	Description
Project ID	AutoNumber	DBMS assigned ID for project
Customer ID	Number	Foreign key link to customer
Name	Text	Project name
Description	Memo	Project description

FIGURE 6-7   Risk Table

Field Name	Data Type	Description
Risk ID	AutoNumber	DBMS assigned ID of project risk
Project ID	Number	Foreign key link to project
Title	Text	Short description of risk
Description	Memo	Long description of risk
Accountable Person	Text	Name of person accountable for risk
Underlying Assumption	Text	Underlying assumption upon which risk is based
Category ID	Number	Foreign key link to category
Severity ID	Number	Foregin key link to severity
Probability ID	Number	Foreign key link to probability
Timeframe ID	Number	Foreign key link to timeframe
Monitoring Metric	Memo	Desciption of the monitoring metric to be used for the risk

FIGURE 6-8   Mitigation Strategy Table

Field Name	Data Type	Description
Mitigation Strategy ID	AutoNumber	DBMS assigned ID for Risk Mitigation Strategy
Risk ID	Number	Foreign key link to project risk
Strategy ID	Number	Foreign key link to risk mitigation strategy type
Title	Text	Title of risk mitigation strategy
Description	Memo	Description of risk mitigation strategy
Implementation Date	Date/Time	Date risk mitigation strategy implemented
Success Metric	Memo	Description of metric to be used to monitor the success or failure of the risk mitigation strategy
Estimated Cost	Currency	Estimated cost in whole dolloars of risk mitigation strategy implementation
Actual Cost	Currency	Actual cost in whole dollars of risk mitigation strategy implementation
Measure	Yes/No	Yes/No answer to success of risk mitigation strategy
Measure Date	Date/Time	Date success/failure of risk mitigation strategy measured
Success-Failure Description	Memo	Description of the success or failure of the risk mitigation strategy

FIGURE 6-9   Contingency Plan Table

Field Name	Data Type	Description
Contingency ID	AutoNumber	DBMS assigned ID of the risk contingency plan
Mitigation Strategy ID	Number	Foreing key link to the risk mitigation strategy
Title	Text	Title of the risk contingency plan
Description	Memo	Description of the risk contingency plan
Trigger	Memo	Description of the condition which will trigger execution of the risk contingency plan
Estimated Cost	Currency	Estimated cost in whole dollars of executing the risk contingnecy plan
Actual Cost	Currency	Actual cost in whole dollars of executing the risk contingnecy plan
Implementation Date	Date/Time	Date risk contingency plan implemented
Measure	Yes/No	Yes/No answer to success of riskcontingency plan
Measure Date	Date/Time	Date success/failure of risk contingency plan measured
Success-Failure Description	Memo	Description of the success or failure of the risk risk contingency plan strategy

Probability

The Probability table indicates the probability of the risk occurring. As described in Chapter 3, risk probability is often defined on a large numerical scale (i.e., 1–10). While each enterprise needs to set its own process, project managers should beware of relying too heavily on numbers and statistics to mitigate risks. A simple low (value = 1), medium (value = 2), and high (value = 3) probability assignment suffices for proactive risk management because the emphasis is on designing proper risk mitigation strategies and contingency plans with appropriate monitoring triggers. Figure 6-10 contains such a Probability table.

Timeframe

The Timeframe table shows when a specific risk may occur. Timeframe is a constantly changing risk. What is a low timeframe risk (e.g., six months from now) will change to a high risk as time passes by. Therefore, it is especially important to ensure that the monitoring trigger for risk be time-sensitive. Figure 6-11 illustrates the attributes of the Timeframe table.

Category

The risk Category table contains information about the category classification of a risk. Chapter 3 defines seven such categories. Each enterprise must examine these categories and modify them for their environment. Risk category provides a convenient classification scheme for future experience-based risk identification. Figure 6-12 outlines the attributes of the risk Category table.

Severity

The risk Severity table, depicted in Figure 6-13, contains information about the predicted severity of risk impact should it occur and not be

FIGURE 6-10   Probability Table

Probability : Table

	Field Name	Data Type	Description
🔑▶	Probability ID	AutoNumber	DBMS assigned ID for Risk Probability
	Probability	Text	Risk Probability name
	Value	Number	Numeric value for risk probability
	Description	Text	Risk Probability description

FIGURE 6-11   Timeframe Table

Timeframe : Table

	Field Name	Data Type	Description
🔑▶	Timeframe ID	AutoNumber	DBMS assigned ID for Risk Timeframe
	Timeframe	Text	Risk Timeframe name
	Value	Number	Numeric value for timeframe risk
	Description	Text	Risk Timeframe description

FIGURE 6-12   Category Table

Category : Table		
Field Name	Data Type	Description
🔑 Category ID	AutoNumber	DBMS assigned ID for Risk Category
Category	Text	Risk category name
Description	Text	Risk category description

FIGURE 6-13   Severity Table

Severity : Table		
Field Name	Data Type	Description
🔑 Severity ID	AutoNumber	DBMS assigned ID for Risk Severity
Severity	Text	Risk Severity name
Value	Number	Numeric value for risk severity
Description	Text	Risk Severity description

mitigated. As with probability, the range of values for probability is less important than ensuring that adequate mitigation strategies and monitoring triggers are established.

Strategy

The Strategy table provides a means of storing information about the type of risk mitigation strategy to be employed. This is another important aspect of information to improve future experience-based risk identification and mitigation. Figure 6-14 illustrates the structure of the Strategy table.

FIGURE 6-14   Strategy Table

Strategy : Table		
Field Name	Data Type	Description
🔑 Strategy ID	AutoNumber	DBMS assigned ID for risk mitigation strategy types
Strategy Type	Text	Risk mitigation strategy type
Description	Memo	Description of risk mitigation strategy

Whatever methods are used to archive information about the success or failure of risk management plans, providing information for future risk management planning activities is of key importance. Too many aspiring project managers have seen their careers snuffed out by failure to mitigate properly the ever-present risks a project brings.

CHAPTER 7

Program Risk Audit

The practice of 'reviewing' . . . in general [has] nothing in common with the art of criticism.

—Henry James

The purpose of the program risk audit is to provide a review and assessment of enterprise-wide planning, preparation, and execution for mitigating the risks of a program of interrelated projects and their issues and problems. The scope of the program audit is at the enterprise level. This will include high-level questions regarding overall project processes but will not include an assessment at the detailed project level. Project level audits occur throughout the execution phase of each project.

The program risk audit has four goals:

- Establishing enterprise-wide views of program status
- Identifying enterprise-wide program risks
- Providing recommendations for risk mitigation improvements
- Minimizing the impact of potential program non-optimal success (i.e., failure).

The techniques used for program risk audits are similar to those used for the project risk audit described in Chapter 4. The primary difference is focus. Program risk audits concentrate on organizational and general management issues.

Because of the cross-functional nature of a program of interrelated projects, the failure of a program can have disastrous consequences for an enterprise. If a single project fails, its sphere of consequences is usually constrained to one functional area of the enterprise. This impact may be severe, but it is usually containable and will not affect the enterprise's overall success. Conversely, when a program fails, the enterprise's overall capability to deliver its products and services may be severely, detrimentally affected. The ultimate result of program failure can be enterprise failure. Therefore, minimizing program failure is a primary concern.

> ### Development of the Program Risk Audit Technique
>
> This technique was initially developed for the State of Washington's Year 2000 Risk Assessment Program and used to assess state agency and university Year 2000 information technology mitigation efforts. Several private consulting firms (Sterling Associates, Cotey Computer Services, CASE Associates, Management Technology Group, and CIBER) worked with the state's Department of Information Services to develop program and project risk assessment criteria and processes. The author modified and extended the process to conduct general program risk audits for non-Y2K programs in the public and private sectors. The technique has proven successful for both information technology and construction projects and is easily adaptable to any program environment.

EXECUTING A PROGRAM RISK AUDIT

Although the techniques used for a program risk audit are parallel to those used for the project risk audit (see Chapter 4), they will be repeated here for clarity. The major difference in the process is the program critical success factors (CSFs) used to evaluate the organizational and management factors of a program of interrelated projects.

Participants

As in a project risk audit, the auditor must be both objective and sensitive to the organizational and management philosophy of the enterprise. Nonetheless, the need for unbiased judgment suggests an external auditor as best practice. If this is not feasible, then a seasoned project manager with substantial quality assurance experience who is not involved with any program project should be selected. The other participants in the audit process and their responsibilities are outlined in Table 7-1.

TABLE 7-1 Program Risk Audit Participants

Participant	Involvement
Program Risk Audit Sponsor	• Establishes the scope of the program risk audit • Ensures cooperation from program sponsors, project teams, and stakeholders
Auditor	• Plans and conducts the program risk audit • Conducts interviews • Analyzes evidence • Prepares findings and recommendations • Presents final audit report
Individual Project Managers	• Participates in interviews • Presents evidence
Executive Program Sponsor(s)	• Participates in interview process
Stakeholders	• Participates in interview process

Timetable

An initial program risk audit should take from 60 to 120 hours over a 10- to 30-day period. Follow-up program risk audits may take less time because they focus on prior audit recommendations and verifying continuing compliance to critical success factor evidentiary requirements. Table 7-2 outlines effort and elapsed time estimates for conducting the program risk audit.

Steps

As shown in Table 7-2, the steps in a program risk audit parallel those of the project risk audit. Figure 7-1 displays a network of the activities involved.

1. **Identifying interviewees**—In a program risk audit, interviews begin at the highest level of an enterprise. Most often, the individuals involved form an executive steering committee responsible for allocating funding and personnel resources to projects. Typical representatives are the chief information officer, chief financial officer, chief operations officer, or their designees. If designees form the executive steering committee, the auditor must determine whether they truly have ultimate decision-making authority for the program under audit review.

2. **Scheduling interviews**—Interviews should be scheduled as soon as possible to solidify the organizational environment aspects of the program. Schedule individual interviews, if possible, to build a

TABLE 7-2 Program Risk Audit Timetable

Task	Effort in Hours	Elapsed Time in Days
Identify interviewees (executive program sponsor(s), significant stakeholders, and individual project managers)	3 – 8	½ – 2
Schedule risk audit interviews	3 – 8	½ – 2
Gather risk audit evidence	8 – 20	2 – 6
Conduct risk audit interviews	8 – 16	2 – 6
Analyze program documentation and interview notes	12 – 20	1½ – 4
Prepare findings	12 – 20	1½ – 4
Prepare recommendations for project risk mitigation	8 – 16	1 – 3
Prepare risk audit report for presentation	6 – 12	1 – 3
Total	60 – 120 hours	10 – 30 days

FIGURE 7-1 Program Risk Audit Process Steps

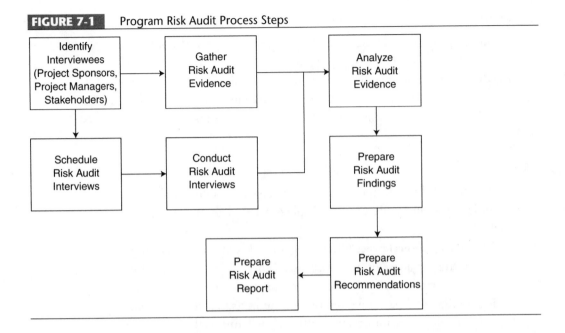

composite picture of organizational factors. Interviews should last approximately one hour each.

3. **Conducting risk audit interviews**—Use the audit working papers (see Figure 7-2) as both a source of interview questions and to record the results. As with a project risk audit, interview notes are the source of referenced evidence; ensure that the interviewee is comfortable with what you record. Either read back interview notes or provide the interviewee with a copy for verification before issuing the risk audit report. For a program audit, interview notes can be considered "hard" evidence.

4. **Gathering risk audit evidence**—Obtain supporting evidence from the program's documentation. Each CSF question on the risk audit instrument specifies the type of documentary evidence needed to demonstrate low risk adequately (see Critical Success Factor section).

5. **Analyzing risk audit evidence**—Analyze the results of the interviews and the content of the collected evidence to determine what risk levels are appropriate for the program (see the Program Risk Audit Evaluation section for a description of the risk rating assessment process).

6. **Preparing risk audit findings**—Document your findings and the associated evidentiary reference.

7. **Preparing risk audit recommendations**—Prepare a recommendation to reduce risk for each CSF (major and subordinate) rated as medium or high risk. Some enterprises may request a "findings only" audit; if so, the risk auditor should see that this is performed. However, having the project management experience required to conduct successful audits places the program risk auditor in an excellent position to make program recommendations for management process improvement.

8. **Preparing the risk audit report**—Prepare the final risk audit report and deliver it to the risk audit sponsor. In addition, the program manager should receive a copy, as he or she will be responsible for responding to the audit and implementing the recommendations.

Deliverables

As with a project risk audit, a major deliverable from the program risk audit process is the risk audit working papers (see Figure 7-2). However,

---

FIGURE 7-2 Extract of Program Risk Audit Working Papers

1. The enterprise is organized to meet its program goals and objectives, scaled to enterprise size.			
1.1. An enterprise-wide program steering committee (or equivalent decision framework) comprised of executive decision makers is functioning.	*Finding:*		
	Recommendation:		
1.2. The enterprise head has designated a program executive sponsor.	*Finding:*		
	Recommendation:		
1.3. An effective enterprise-wide program (or functional equivalent) organization has been defined.	*Finding:*		
	Recommendation:		
1.4. The enterprise is organized to meet its program goals and objectives, scaled to enterprise size.	*Finding:*		
	Recommendation:		

take great caution when distributing these. The working papers reference both interview and documentary evidence. Interview evidence plays a more important role in program risk audits than in project risk audits. In addition, program risk audits focus closely on internal enterprise organizational factors and are therefore more politically explosive. As such, interview evidence should remain confidential.

During the planning process for a program risk audit, ensure that working paper distribution and confidentiality agreements are established and closely followed. Because an enterprise-wide program tends to cross "silos" of function, middle management may feel threatened. Under threat, a common human reaction is to withdraw into a turtle-like shell or to take the position of an ostrich with its head buried in the sand. Therefore, because an auditor's ability to discern risk-based information often rests on his or her credibility with the interviewee, interview confidentiality is of great concern. If an interviewee feels threatened by auditor exposure, he or she may not be forthcoming, which will lead to "covered up" risks. **Remember: the purpose of a program risk audit is to reduce risk and improve the probability of program success, *not* to point fingers!**

In addition to the risk audit working papers, a number of other supporting documents are produced during the risk audit process:

- **Interview log** containing interview control number for reference in risk audit working papers, interview date, interviewee name and title, and interviewer name.
- **Documentation log** containing document control number for reference in risk audit working papers, a brief description of the document content, reviewer's name, and a reviewed-by date.
- **Audit summary** of the sub-CSF level audit content summarizing the findings, assessment rating, and recommendations for the ten CSFs.

In traditional audit scenarios, the auditor, at the discretion of the audit sponsor, presents only findings. However, one of the essential characteristics of program risk auditors is their experience in successfully completing projects. Therefore, encourage the audit sponsor to agree to recommendations for improvement and risk reduction.

PROGRAM RISK AUDIT EVALUATION

As with the project risk audit described in Chapter 4, the program risk audit uses a set of ten CSFs to evaluate the effectiveness (i.e., riskiness) of management, planning, resourcing, and other processes essential to a program's success:

1. **Organization**—The enterprise is organized to meet its program goals and objectives, scaled to enterprise size.
2. **Planning**—The enterprise has planned for its program.
3. **Financial resources**—Sufficient financial resources (macro-level assessment) have been budgeted.
4. **Direction**—The enterprise is providing clear direction to its program and projects.
5. **Coordination**—The enterprise is coordinating its program efforts.
6. **Communication**—The enterprise is effectively communicating its program status and issues.
7. **Staffing resources**—The enterprise has devoted sufficient (macro-level assessment) program and technical staff to its program and projects.
8. **Control**—The enterprise is controlling its program and projects.
9. **Risk assessment**—The enterprise is fully aware of the program issues and risks.
10. **Seeks remedies**—The enterprise recognizes when it needs help and actively pursues remedies.

Each critical success factor divides into sub-CSFs providing detailed evaluation questions and assessment criteria. Depending on the program type and environment, the subfactors defining each critical success factor may require modification or extension. Assign assessment ratings using a simple three-level system: high, medium, and low risk. Apply the following rating definitions for the assessment:

- **High**—There is a high likelihood that the enterprise's program to mitigate the disruption of enterprise operations will not be effective. Immediate executive attention is required.
- **Medium**—There is a moderate likelihood that the enterprise's program to mitigate the disruption of enterprise operations will not be effective. Internal management attention is required.
- **Low**—There is little likelihood that the enterprise's program to mitigate the disruption of enterprise operations will not be effective. Corroborating evidence clearly supports this determination. Continued enterprise management attention is required.

Document the findings for the sub-CSFs with appropriate references to supporting interview notes or other documentation (e.g., cataloged evidence). After analyzing the sub-CSFs, assign an overall assessment rating. To provide a moderately conservative risk audit, use the following guidelines (detailed in Table 7-3) for each major critical success factor rating:

- If one-half or more of the sub-CSFs are high risk, rate the CSF as high risk.
- If three-quarters or more of the sub-CSFs are low risk and there are no high-risk ratings, assign the CSF a low-risk rating.
- Rate any other combination as medium risk.

In extreme situations in which program process failure would have disastrous results, a more conservative approach for rating evaluation is justifiable. That is, if at least one sub-CSF assesses as high risk, then the CSF is at high risk. If at least one sub-CSF assesses as medium risk with no high-risk sub-CSFs, then the CSF is medium risk. Finally, if and only if *all* sub-CSFs are low risk may the CSF be assessed as low risk.

As well as establishing a rating for the major critical success factors, you should create a recommendation for action to reduce risk for each high- or medium-risk sub-CSF.

Use a similar strategy to rate the overall program risk (see Table 7-4). If five or more main CSFs are high, the overall rating is high. If seven or more CSFs are low and there are no highs, the rating is low. Any other combination is rated as medium risk.

This technique requires little training and no program-specific knowledge. A typical initial risk audit can be completed in 60 to 120 hours of effort, depending on the availability of necessary interviewees, the state of program documentation, and the required level of reference documentation

TABLE 7-3 Individual CSF Rating Evaluation

| Critical Success Factor | # Sub-CSFs | Critical Success Factor Rating | | |
		Low	Medium	High
Organization	4	0 High & ≥ 3 Low	1 High or < 3 Low	≥ 2 High
Planning	5	0 High & ≥ 4 Low	1 High or < 4 Low	≥ 4 High
Financial Resources	2	2 Low	1 High or < 2 Low	≥ 1 High
Direction	3	0 High & ≥ 2 Low	1 High or < 2 Low	≥ 2 High
Coordination	2	2 Low	1 High or < 2 Low	≥ 1 High
Communication	4	0 High & ≥ 3 Low	1 High or < 3 Low	≥ 2 High
Staffing Resources	8	0 High & ≥ 6 Low	1 High or < 6 Low	≥ 4 High
Control	4	0 High & ≥ 3 Low	1 High or < 3 Low	≥ 2 High
Risk Assessment	4	0 High & ≥ 3 Low	1 High or < 3 Low	≥ 2 High
Seeks Remedies	3	0 High & ≥ 2 Low	1 High or < 2 Low	≥ 2 High

TABLE 7-4 Overall CSF Rating

Individual CSF Ratings			
Low	Medium	High	Overall Rating
≥ 7	—	0	Low
—	≥ 6	≤ 4	Medium
—	—	≥ 5	High
—	Number Irrelevant		

and supporting evidence. Follow-up risk audits require less time because open recommendations on high and medium critical success factors become the focus of evaluation.

As with the project risk audit, the technique concentrates on the "correctness" of the risk audit rather than on a numerical rating system. The findings and recommendations form the core of the technique. That is, while it is important to identify the risk level and even boldly display it in color on presentations (i.e., high = red, medium = yellow, and low = green), the principal value is in the recommended corrective actions to reduce risk and better ensure success.

As stated, provide supporting evidence for the findings, such as interview notes and actual documentation. It is essential to be objective when evaluating evidence. Just as in a financial audit, the feelings and impressions of the auditor are not important. Findings represent a summary gathered from referenced evidence. Document evidence references in the audit working papers (see Figure 7-2).

PROGRAM RISK AUDIT CRITICAL SUCCESS FACTORS

The ten program audit CSFs are detailed below. As stated, each major CSF is broken into multiple sub-CSFs. The CSF tables detail the sub-CSFs, provide instructions for their evaluation, and, where appropriate, emphasize the type of evidence that should be present to justify a low CSF rating evaluation (see Tables 7-5 through 7-14).

Organization (CSF #1)

This CSF examines how the enterprise is organized to support and effectively monitor enterprise-wide programs of projects. Without sufficient program organization it will be difficult, if not impossible, to deal effectively

TABLE 7-5 Program Organization (CSF #1)

Critical Success Factor	Instructions	Criteria/Acceptable Evidence
1. The enterprise is organized to meet its program goals and objectives, scaled to enterprise size.	If 2 or more sub-categories are HIGH, this score is HIGH. If 3 or more sub-categories are LOW, and there are no HIGHs, this score is LOW. Any other combination is MEDIUM.	• Program organization chart
1.2. An enterprise-wide program steering committee (or equivalent decision framework) comprised of executive decision makers is functioning.	• Explain the steering committee (or equivalent) organization, membership, roles, and responsibilities. • What have been the issues to date, and how have they been resolved?	• Program executive steering committee charter • Program executive steering committee minutes
1.3. The enterprise head has designated a program executive sponsor.	• Who is the executive sponsor, and how is that person involved in the enterprise program effort?	• Program executive steering committee charter
1.4. An effective enterprise-wide program (or functional equivalent) organization has been defined.	• Has a program office (or functional equivalent) been created and staffed? (Explain) • How is your program (or equivalent) organized? (Explain)	• Program organization chart
1.5. Customer organization program management roles and responsibilities, with lines of authority and accountability, have been defined and agreed upon.	• Have the roles and responsibilities been clearly defined and agreed upon? (Explain the process and what they are) • Have lines of authority and accountability been clearly defined and agreed upon? (Explain the process and what they are)	• Program executive steering committee charter

with inter-project issues and priorities. Individual program project success, while important in itself, must be subordinate to the larger program goals and objectives.

Planning (CSF #2)

The Planning CSF examines whether or not sufficient program level planning was completed. Program plans deal with the interrelationships of the individual projects and are critical to ensuring that interfaces and dependencies are dealt with properly.

TABLE 7-6 Program Planning (CSF #2)

Critical Success Factor	Instructions	Criteria/ Acceptable Evidence
2. The enterprise has planned for its program.	If 4 or more sub-categories are HIGH, this score is HIGH. If 6 or more sub-categories are LOW, and there are no HIGHs, this score is LOW. Any other combination is MEDIUM.	• Tactical plans related to the program
2.1. Prioritization criteria have been established.	• Have prioritization criteria been developed? (Do they involve services and information systems?) • What was the process for developing the criteria? • Have prioritization criteria been approved, and by whom? (What was the process?) • Is there a process for ongoing prioritization? (Explain)	• Prioritization criteria for mitigation to services and systems affected by program problems
2.2. Services and systems have been prioritized against the criteria.	• Have services and systems been prioritized against the criteria? • Explain the process of prioritizing.	• Process for applying mitigation criteria
2.3. An enterprise-wide program plan has been developed.	• Has an enterprise-wide program plan been developed? (Discuss) • What are the contents of the plan?	• Program description, plan, and charter
2.4. A program assessment has been completed for significant at-risk business processes and systems.	• What kinds of program assessments have been completed for significant at-risk business processes and systems? • Who was involved in the assessments? • Were the results documented?	• Results of individual business and system program assessments
2.5. Project plans have been developed and approved by enterprise management for each program project.	• Have project plans been developed for each program project? • Have the plans been approved (and if so, by whom)?	• Documented program project plans
2.6. Contingency plans have been developed for each program project.	• Have contingency plans been developed for each project? (Explain) • Do the contingency plans mitigate disruption to services? (Explain)	• Contingency plans for program projects
2.7. System capacity requirements and forecasts have been defined.	• Have system internal and external capacity requirements and forecasts been defined? (Explain how accomplished)	• System capacity requirements for program efforts
2.8. Dependencies within and among program projects have been defined and are included in the enterprise-wide program.	• Is there an overall plan to monitor and coordinate individual projects? • Are dependencies defined? (Explain process) • How are these dependencies being managed, tracked, and monitored? • How are issues involving dependencies handled/decided?	• Overall program project plan to monitor and coordinate individual plans

Financial Resources (CSF #3)

This factor checks the financial resources that have been budgeted for the program. Basically, this is the sum of the individual project budgets and funds to ensure proper integration of the projects. The assessment examines

TABLE 7-7 Program Financial Resources (CSF #3)

Critical Success Factor	Instructions	Criteria/Acceptable Evidence
3. **Sufficient financial resources have been budgeted (macro level assessment).**	If 1 or more sub-categories are HIGH, this score is HIGH. If 2 sub-categories are LOW, this score is LOW. Any other combination is MEDIUM.	• High-level financial resource estimates
3.1. Financial resource estimates have been made for significant program projects.	• Have financial resource estimates been made for significant projects? (Explain process)	• Individual project budgets
3.2. Customer organization budgeted resources are sufficient (at macro level) to meet program and project requirements.	• What is the estimated budget for the enterprise's program and projects? • How was this estimated? • How confident is the enterprise that this budget is sufficient? (Why or why not?)	• Program budget

TABLE 7-8 Program Direction (CSF #4)

Critical Success Factor	Instructions	Criteria/Acceptable Evidence
4. **The enterprise is providing clear direction to its program and projects.**	If 2 or more sub-categories are HIGH, this score is HIGH. If 2 or more sub-categories are LOW, and there are no HIGHs, this score is LOW. Any other combination is MEDIUM.	• Program charter
4.1. Executives are committed to the success of the enterprise's program.	• Is the program getting sufficient attention from enterprise executives? (Explain why or how)	• Program committee charters
4.2. Program standards have been developed and established.	• Have program standards been developed? (Explain or provide copy) • Do they include change control, testing, configuration management, scope of changes, coordination with maintenance and production staff, project management, etc.?	• Program standards • Change management, configuration management, and testing process definitions
4.7. A program issue management process has been adopted and is functional.	• Explain your issue management process. • Is the process working?	• Issue management process • Program issue resolution logs

the financial resources at a macro level. At this level, it is not necessary to assess earned value or variance, but rather to assess that financial resource estimates are available and justifiable.

Direction (CSF #4)

This CSF judges the direction that program management is applying to the program projects. It assesses the processes that are in place to ensure that proper attention is given to individual projects, that necessary program-level standards have been established, and that program issue management is effectively established.

Coordination (CSF #5)

The Program Coordination CSF assesses the effectiveness of program management in synchronizing the efforts of the individual program projects, examining internal and external interfaces, and coordinating among enterprise business units and external entities.

TABLE 7-9 Program Coordination (CSF #5)

Critical Success Factor	Instructions	Criteria/Acceptable Evidence
5. **The enterprise is coordinating its program efforts.**	If 1 or more sub-categories are HIGH, this score is HIGH. If 2 sub-categories are LOW, this score is LOW. Any other combination is MEDIUM.	• Program charter
5.1. Internal and external system interfaces are understood and coordinated.	• Have internal and external system interfaces been identified? • How many *internal* interfaces have been identified? • How many *external* interfaces have been identified? • How are the interface issues being coordinated?	• Internal and external interface documentation
5.2. Program projects are coordinated with appropriate entities.	Are program projects coordinated with (as applicable and needed): • Business units? • Other affected systems? • Customer organization information services organization? • Direct service suppliers and providers? • Data and telecommunications service providers? • Hardware and software vendors?	• Internal and external coordination plans

Communication (CSF #6)

This CSF examines how program management handles communications. It assesses the program's communication plan, status-reporting process, and method of documenting decisions.

Staffing Resources (CSF #7)

This factor assesses the program resource requirements and project managers to see if they are sufficient and capable of completing project work. The auditor evaluates how program management addresses resource shortages, if any.

TABLE 7-10 Program Communication (CSF #6)

Critical Success Factor	Instructions	Criteria/Acceptable Evidence
6. The enterprise is effectively communicating its program status and issues.	If 2 or more sub-categories are HIGH, this score is HIGH. If 3 or more sub-categories are LOW, and there are no HIGHs, this score is LOW. Any other combination is MEDIUM.	
6.1. A program communications plan has been developed.	• Has the enterprise developed a communications plan for internal and external stakeholders? • Does the plan communicate the importance of mitigation to disruption of services?	• Program communication plan
6.2. Program project status is accurately reported on a frequent basis to project sponsor and other internal stakeholders.	• What is the process for reporting project status? To whom and how often?	• Program project status reports
6.3. Customer organization-wide program status is reported accurately to executives, business managers, and appropriate stakeholders.	• How is program status (overall state of the enterprise's program effort) reported? To whom and how often?	• Program status reports
6.4. Enterprise is documenting decisions and processes to support program mitigation strategies.	• Have decisions and processes been documented? • Are documentation standards in place for program mitigation efforts?	• Decision documentation

TABLE 7-11 Program Staffing Resources (CSF #7)

Critical Success Factor	Instructions	Criteria/Acceptable Evidence
7. The enterprise has devoted sufficient (macro level assessment) program and technical staff to its program and projects.	If 4 or more sub-categories are HIGH, this score is HIGH. If 6 or more sub-categories are LOW, and there are no HIGHs, this score is LOW. Any other combination is MEDIUM.	
7.1. The enterprise's ability and capacity have been examined to meet resource requirements.	• Have the enterprise's ability (required skills) and capacity (enough) to meet resource requirements been examined? (Explain process) • Does this include requirements for staff, space, equipment, etc.?	• Ability and capacity assessments for program project efforts
7.2. Alternative remediation sources have been examined and retained to compensate for any internal shortages.	• What additional resources have been retained to compensate for internal shortages? (Explain) • What additional resources are still needed? (Explain what and why)	• Documentation of requirements for additional resources • Documentation of how resource shortages are resolved
7.3. The enterprise has acquired tools and adopted processes to support program projects.	• Explain the tools and processes to support program projects at the enterprise level.	• List of tools being used or planned to be used
7.4. Program project managers are qualified.	• How are the project managers qualified? (Have they managed projects before? • Do they understand the unique issues involved in program efforts?	• Project manager qualification assessments
7.5. Staff estimates have been made for each significant program project.	• Have staff estimates been made for each significant program project? (If not all, how many?) • How were these estimates accomplished, and what were they based upon?	• Staffing estimates for program projects
7.6. Staff are competent as a result of training or experience in appropriate processes and tools.	• Have staff been trained and how? • Are the staff competent (in the enterprise's opinion) for their assignments?	• Training needs or other documents related to ability and capacity
7.7. Program and technical staff commitments to projects are enforced.	• Are they enforced, and how?	• Documentation regarding commitments of staff • Policies to mitigate turnover
7.8. Management and staff turnover is minimized.	• How is management and staff turnover minimized? • Have there been occurrences of staff turnover?	• Documentation regarding commitments of staff • Policies to mitigate turnover • Documentation related to staff turnover

Control (CSF #8)

The Control CSF considers how program management exercises control over key resources availability and examines program testing processes and tools. Moreover, and more important for highly critical or risky programs, the auditor assesses how quality assurance is implemented.

Risk Assessment (CSF #9)

The Risk Assessment CSF examines how program management copes with program risk. The auditor assesses risk awareness within program management and business units affected by the program. The inventory of an at-risk business process is checked to ensure that adequate risk mitigation is in place.

TABLE 7-12 Program Control (CSF #8)

	Critical Success Factor	Instructions	Criteria/Acceptable Evidence
8.	The enterprise is controlling its program and projects.	If 2 or more sub-categories are HIGH, this score is HIGH. If 3 or more sub-categories are LOW, and there are no HIGHs, this score is LOW. Any other combination is MEDIUM.	
8.1.	Measures are in place to ensure the availability of key resources	• What controls are in place to ensure availability of key resources?	• Key resource requirements documentation
8.2.	System testing processes and tools are identified and used.	• Explain the system testing processes and tools that are identified and will be used.	• Testing process documentation
8.3.	Sufficient (macro-level assessment) resources have been identified and assigned for program testing.	• Have staff resources been identified and assigned for program testing? • Have computing resources been identified and assigned for program testing?	• Testing plans with resource allocation
8.4.	Independent quality assurance is provided over significant program projects.	• Is independent (internal or external) quality assurance provided for significant program projects? (Explain)	• Quality assurance policy and process

TABLE 7-13 Program Risk Assessment (CSF #9)

	Critical Success Factor	Instructions	Criteria/Acceptable Evidence
9.	**The enterprise is fully aware of the program issues and risks.**	If 2 or more sub-categories are HIGH, this score is HIGH. If 3 or more sub-categories are LOW, and there are no HIGHs, this score is LOW. Any other combination is MEDIUM.	• Strategic technology plan
9.1.	The enterprise director and management team are fully aware of program issues and risks.	• How will program issues impact the enterprise? • What are the most significant risks to the enterprise's service delivery that must be mitigated? • How are the program risk issues being addressed? (Through what forum? Management goals? Business plans?)	• Business plan
9.2.	Business units have examined key business processes for program risks and implications.	• How have key business processes been examined for program risks and implications? • How was that process accomplished? (How and who) • Is there a process in place for ongoing assessments? (Explain)	• Business plan
9.3.	A complete inventory of at-risk business processes and systems exists.	• Is there an inventory of at-risk business processes and systems? • How was the inventory process accomplished?	• Business plan • Inventory of business processes affected by the program • Inventory of at-risk business processes
9.4.	The probability and severity of potential failures have been determined.	• Have the probability and severity of potential information systems failures been determined? (Ultimate impact to services) • If so, how was probability determined? • If so, how was severity determined?	• Business process risk assessment results (probability and severity of potential impacts on service delivery)

Seeks Remedies (CSF #10)

This CSF examines how program management resolves situations requiring remedy. The key factors to assess are how the enterprise recognizes situations requiring remedy, how it resolves those situations, and how it justifies the remedy solution.

TABLE 7-14 Program Seeks Remedies (CSF #10)

Critical Success Factor	Instructions	Criteria/Acceptable Evidence
10. The enterprise recognizes when it needs help and actively pursues remedies.	If 2 or more sub-categories are HIGH, this score is HIGH. If 2 or more sub-categories are LOW, and there is no HIGH, this score is LOW. Any other combination is MEDIUM.	
10.1. The enterprise monitors conditions for early awareness of the need for additional remedies.	• How are program and project conditions monitored to ensure assistance needs are recognized, sought, and provided on time?	• Issue management process
10.2. When necessary, the enterprise actively seeks remedies. (Indicate if not applicable)	• What kinds of needs has the enterprise had, and how and where has it pursued remedies? • How has the enterprise attempted to get help or solve the problem internally? • Who has this need been discussed with? • If needed, has a budget request been defined and presented or planned for supplemental funding?	• Documentation relating to seeking additional resources or remedies for mitigating program risks
10.3. The enterprise can justify its request for help or additional remedies. (Indicate if not applicable)	• Is the need for formal help clearly substantiated and documented? • What have been the significant barriers (if any) to recognizing, finding, and getting help or obtaining remedies? • Does the enterprise trust that its requests will be treated fairly and constructively?	• Documentation relating to seeking additional resources or remedies for mitigating program risks

Program risk audits are less common than project risk audits. However, as enterprises move toward project-based efforts, it will become increasingly apparent that they are as interrelated as business processes. Moreover, enterprise survival requires that all projects are completed successfully.

A program risk audit provides an independent assessment of an enterprise's capability to manage a program of projects. The audit findings and, most important, the recommendations provide an enterprise with the information necessary to establish proper, best-practice standards and processes. Once instituted, these processes will reduce the risk of surprise and failure.

Bibliography

Chapman, C. B., and S. C. Ward. *Project Risk Management: Processes, Techniques and Insights* (New York: John Wiley & Sons, Inc., 1996).

Grey, S. *Practical Risk Assessment for Project Management* (New York: John Wiley & Sons, Inc., 1995).

Hall, Elaine M. *Managing Risk—Methods for Software Systems Development* (Boston, MA: Addison Wesley Longman, 1998).

Jones, Capers. *Assessment and Control of Software Risks* (Upper Saddle River, NJ: Yourdon Press Prentice Hall, 1994).

Karolak, Dale Walter. *Software Engineering Risk Management* (Los Alamitos, CA: The Computer Society Press, 1996).

Kerzner, Harold. *In Search of Excellence in Project Management* (New York: John Wiley & Sons, Inc., 1998).

Kliem, R. L., and I. S. Ludin. *Reducing Project Risk* (Abingdon Oxon, UK: Gower Publishing, 1997).

Koller, Glenn. *Risk Assessment and Decision Making in Business and Industry: A Practical Guide* (Boca Raton, FL: CRC Press, Inc., 1999).

Krantz, L., and A. Thomason. *Strategic Investment Decisions: Harnessing Opportunities, Managing Risks* (Upper Saddle River, NJ: Financial Times/ Prentice Hall, 1999).

Megill, Robert E. *An Introduction to Risk Analysis* (Tulsa, OK: PennWell Publishing Co., 1984).

Project Management Institute. *A Guide to the Project Management Body of Knowledge* (*PMBOK® Guide—2000 Edition*) (Newton Square, PA: Project Management Institute, 2000).

Royer, Paul S. How Healthy Is Your Project? (Project Management Institute: PMI® Symposium 2000 Proceedings, September 2000).

Royer, Paul S. Risk Management: The Undiscovered Dimension of Project Management. *PM Journal* 31(1), 2000.

Wideman, R. Max. *Project and Program Risk Management: A Guide to Managing Risks and Opportunities* (Upper Darby, PA: Project Management Institute, 1992).

Risk Management Lexicon

This risk management lexicon was compiled in June 1998 by the Project Management Institute's Risk Special Interest Group. A current list can be found at its Website: www.risksig.com.

acceptance/accepted risk—An approach that does nothing with a risk, but rather prepares for and deals with the consequences of a risk should it occur. No risk management resources are expended dealing with accepted risks. See *acceptance rationale*.

acceptance rationale—A type of action plan that documents the reason for accepting a risk (doing nothing with it). This is documented for historical reasons.

acquisition—The process of obtaining through contract.

(*system*) acquisition management personnel—Those individuals who are trained, educated, or experienced in acquisition management and who are either assigned to or support the project team in the performance of acquisition activities.

acquisition organization—That entity which has the oversight responsibility for the acquisition project and which may have purview over the acquisition activities of a number of projects or contract actions.

acquisition organization's standard acquisition process—The acquisition organization's fundamental acquisition process which guides the establishment of each project's defined acquisition process.

acquisition plans—The collection of plans, both formal and informal, used to express how acquisition activities will be performed; for example, the Acquisition Risk Management Plan or Project Management Plan.

acquisition process—A set of activities, methods, practices, and transformations that people use to acquire a system and the associated products.

(*project's defined*) acquisition process—The project's tailored version of the acquisition organization's standard acquisition process.

acquisition process assets—A collection of entities, maintained by an organization, for use by projects in developing, tailoring, maintaining, and implementing their acquisition processes. Some examples of these acquisition process assets include:
- the acquisition organization's standard acquisition process,
- descriptions of the lifecycles approved for use the guidelines and criteria for tailoring the acquisition organization's standard acquisition process,
- the organization's acquisition process database,
- a library of acquisition process-related documentation

- any entity that the organization considers useful in performing the activities of process definition and maintenance could be included as a process asset.

acquisition process group—The group responsible for the definition, improvement, and maintenance of the acquisition organization's standard acquisition process and related process assets, including guidelines for all projects to tailor the standard acquisition process to their specific situations. It coordinates process activities with the projects and related elements of the organization.

acquisition process-related documentation—Documents and document fragments that may be of use to future project teams when tailoring the acquisition organization's standard acquisition process. The examples may cover subjects such as a project's defined acquisition process, standards, procedures, acquisition risk management plans, and training materials.

acquisition process repository—A collection of acquisition process information (e.g., estimated and actual data on project size, effort, and cost; and project team productivity and quality data) gathered from the acquisition projects that is maintained by the acquisition organization to support its acquisition definition and improvement activities.

acquisition project—An undertaking that is focused on acquiring the components and associated documentation of a system.

acquisition-related group—A collection of individuals (both managers and technical staff) representing a discipline that supports, but is not directly responsible for, acquisition. Examples of disciplines include configuration management and quality assurance.

action—This is an activity which management may decide to implement with the intention of mitigating a risk (reducing Probability and/or Impact) or enhancing an opportunity (increasing Probability and/or Impact). The activity and its associated cost are independent of the actual occurrence of the task.

activity—Any step taken or function performed, either mental or physical, toward achieving some objective of a project. Activities include all the work the managers and technical staff do to perform the tasks of the project and organization. Activities have expected duration, costs and resource requirements, and may be subdivided into tasks.

analyze/analysis—A process in which risks are examined in further detail to determine the extent of the risks, how they relate to each other, and which ones are the most important to deal with. Analyzing risks has three basic activities:
- evaluating the attributes of risks
- classifying risks
- prioritizing (ranking) risks

application domain—A bounded set of related systems (i.e., systems that address a particular type of problem). Development and maintenance in an application domain usually require special skills and/or resources. Examples include payroll and personnel systems, avionics, command and control systems, compilers, and expert systems.

attributes—Characteristics such as reliability, maintainability, portability, and complexity. These characteristics are sometimes referred to as quality attributes.

avoidance—A mitigation strategy that eliminates the threat of a specific risk, usually by eliminating its potential cause. See *acceptance* and *mitigation.*

baseline—A specification or product that has been formally reviewed and agreed upon, that thereafter serves as the basis for further development, and that can be changed only through formal change control procedures [IEEE-STD-610].

baseline assessment—The initial set of probability and impact assessments. These are usually the assessments made when risks are first identified. These assessments are usually maintained in the project log to support prioritization, progress measurement, expected value/state determination, etc. Initial assessments describe risks under the initial baseline plan for the project, and may indicate areas for needed risk (project) management. Since risk management is an iterative process, subsequent events, risk management actions and new information will always change the assessment which will ultimately be adopted as the baseline. A Project Manager should look at the risk analysis results and conduct risk management before adopting a baseline plan.

capability maturity model (CMM)—A description of the stages through which organizations evolve as they define, implement, measure, control, and improve their processes. The model provides a guide for selecting process improvement strategies by facilitating the determination of current process capabilities and the identification of the issues most critical to quality and process improvement.

commitment—A pact that is freely assumed, visible, and expected to be kept by all parties.

communicate/communication—A process in which risk information is conveyed between all levels of a project team. Risk communication deals with transferring knowledge and awareness of risk probability, consequences, and opportunity and mitigation plans and actions. It is essential for the management of risks within an organization. Communication must both fit within an organization's culture and expose the risks that are present in an organization's projects.

condition—The key circumstances, situations, etc., that are causing concern, doubt, anxiety, or uncertainty. In a risk statement, the condition phrase is the phrase at the beginning of the statement.

consequence—The possible negative outcomes of the current conditions that are creating uncertainty. In a risk statement, the consequence phrase is the phrase at the end of the statement.

consistency—The degree of uniformity, standardization, and freedom from contradiction among the documents or parts of a system or component [IEEE-STD-610].

context—Context provides additional detail regarding the events, circumstances, and interrelationships within the project that may affect the risk. This description is more detailed than can be captured in the basic statement of risk.

contingency plan—The process of identifying and planning appropriate responses to be taken when, and if, a risk actually occurs. See *management reserve.*

continuous risk management—An engineering practice with processes, methods, and tools for managing risks in a project. It provides a disciplined environment for proactive decision-making to:

- assess continuously what could go wrong (risks)
- determine which risks are important to deal with
- implement strategies to deal with those risks

contract—A binding agreement between two or more parties that establishes the requirements for the products and services to be acquired.

contract integrity—The adherence and compliance to contractual and legal policies, regulations, and other guidance.

contract terms and conditions—The stated legal, financial, and administrative aspects of a contract.

contractor—The entity delivering the product or performing the service being acquired, even if that entity is part of the acquiring organization.

control—A process that takes the tracking status reports for the watched and mitigated project risks and decides what to do with them based on the reported data. The person who has accountability for a risk normally makes the control decision for that risk.

The general process of controlling risks includes:
- analyzing the status reports
- deciding how to proceed
- executing the decisions

critical path—The series of activities that determine the earliest completion of a project.

critical path method (CPM)—A technique used to predict project duration by analyzing the sequence of activities (path) that has the least amount of scheduling flexibility.

current assessment—The most current set of probability and impact assessments. One reason that the current assessment may be different from the baseline assessment is the implementation of proactive actions. However, the current assessment may also change just due to the passage of time, the availability of new information, a change in the project's environment risk mitigation actions, etc.

decision analysis—The discipline of assessing the value of alternative actions on the project taking into account the costs of taking the action, the likelihood of future uncertain actions that may occur if the action is taken, and the rewards or costs estimated to result. The decision made is usually the one which yields the greatest expected value (or the least expected cost).

defined level—See *maturity level*

defined acquisition process—See *acquisition process*

effectiveness—A measure of the favorable effect of implementing one or more risk management actions.

end user—The individual or group who will use the system for its intended operational use when it is deployed in its environment.

end user representatives—A selected sample of end users who represent the total population of end users.

evaluation—The use of reviews, inspections, and/or tests, to determine that a product or service satisfies specified requirements.

event-driven review—A review that is performed based on the occurrence of an event within the project (e.g., a formal review or the completion of a lifecycle stage). See *periodic review* for contrast.

expected value—For quantitative assessments only. It is the product of probability and impact. If the impact is stated probabilistically, then the mean of the distribution is commonly used in the calculation. Since probability is a dimensionless number, the units and sign of expected value are the same as the units and sign of the impact. The expected value is computed by weighting all possible outcomes (e.g., possible element costs, possible activity durations) by their relative likelihood of occurring. If discrete scenarios are anticipated, their results would be weighted by the likelihood (summing to 100%) of occurring. If a continuous probability distribution is used, a mean value can usually be found. Monte Carlo simulation will compute this value.

findings—The statements or facts from an assessment, evaluation, audit, or review. An assessment, evaluation, audit, or review includes conclusions which are drawn from the findings by applying expert judgment that identify the most important issues, problems, or opportunities within the area of investigation.

function—A set of related *activities*, undertaken by individuals or tools that are specifically assigned or fitted for their roles, to accomplish a set purpose or end.

group—An assemblage of personnel organized to serve a specific purpose or accomplish a task. A group may vary from a single individual assigned part time, to several part-time individuals assigned from other organizations, to several individuals dedicated full-time.

identify—A process of transforming uncertainties and issues about the project into distinct (tangible) risks that can be described and measured. Identifying risks involves two activities:
- capturing a statement of risk
- capturing the context of a risk

impact—The loss or effect on the project if the risk occurs. Impact is one of the three attributes of a risk. A risk that does not affect an objective is not particularly important to a project manager. A risk that can affect the objective should be assessed and, if possible, its impact quantified. Qualitative judgments such as low, moderate and high risk impacts are useful in some cases. The impact is traditionally described in two dimensions, its likelihood of occurring and the impact on an objective should it occur."
- Qualitative Assessment—The "IMPACT" is stated in qualitative units such as None, Low, Medium and High.
- Quantitative Assessment—The units of "IMPACT" are flexible. Examples include: Monetary ($, Yen, etc.), Time (Days, Weeks, etc.), Performance (Efficiency, speed, etc.).

initial level—See *maturity level*

institutionalization—The building of infrastructure and corporate culture that supports methods, practices, and procedures so that they are the ongoing way of doing business, even after those who originally defined them are gone.

insurable risk—Risk that can be covered by an insurance policy.

lessons learned—Documented information usually collected through meetings, discussions or written reports, to show both common and uncommon project events were addressed.

lifecycle—The period of time that begins when a product is conceived and ends when the (*product*) is no longer available for use. The lifecycle typically includes a concept phase, requirements phase, design phase, implementation phase, test phase, installation and checkout phase, operation and maintenance phase, and, sometimes, retirement phase.

managed and controlled—Implies that the version of the work product in use at a given time (past or present) is known (i.e., version control), and changes are incorporated in a controlled manner (i.e., change control).

management reserve—Separately planned quantity of money or time intended to reduce the impact of missed cost, schedule, or performance objectives, which are impossible to plan for.

manager—A role that encompasses providing technical and administrative direction and control to individuals performing tasks or activities within the manager's area of responsibility. The traditional functions of a manager include planning, resourcing, organizing, directing, and controlling work within an area of responsibility.

maturity level—A well-defined evolutionary plateau toward achieving a mature process. (e.g., the five maturity levels in the SA-CMM are *Initial, Repeatable, Defined, Quantitative,* and *Optimizing.*)

measure—To ascertain the characteristics or features (extent, dimension, quantity, capacity, and capability) of something, especially by comparing with a standard.

measurement—The dimension, capacity, quantity, or amount of something (e.g., 300 source lines of code or seven document pages of design).

method—A reasonably complete set of rules and criteria that establish a precise and repeatable way of performing a task and arriving at a desired result.

methodology—A collection of methods, procedures, and standards that defines an integrated synthesis of approaches.

milestone—1. A task with zero duration and requiring no resources, that is used to measure the progress of a project and signifies completion or start of a major deliverable, 2. Identifiable point in a project or set of activities that represents a reporting requirement or completion of a large or important set of activities.

mitigate—An approach that deals with a risk by developing strategies and actions for reducing (or eliminating) the impact, probability, or both, of the risk to some acceptable level. It may also involve shifting the time frame when action must be taken. See mitigation plan.

mitigation—A strategy that decreases risk by lowering the probability of a risk event's occurrence or reducing the effect of the risk should it occur. See also *acceptance* and *avoidance.*

mitigation approach—The approach taken to deal with a risk. This can be to accept it, research it, watch it, or mitigate it.

mitigation costs—Those costs directly associated with mitigating specific risks to the project. This is the cost of carrying out the mitigation plan.

mitigation plan—An action plan for risks that are to be mitigated. It documents the strategies, actions, goals, schedule dates, tracking requirements, and all other supporting information needed to carry out the mitigation strategy.

mitigation strategy—See *mitigation plan*

Monte Carlo analysis—A technique in which outcomes of events are determined by selecting random numbers subject to defined probabilities. The process is done on an iterative basis to determine statistical likelihood.

odds—The ratio of probabilities of occurrence and non-occurrence. (e.g., the odds of getting a 4 on the throw of a single die are 5 to 1.)

offeror—A contractor who submits a proposal in response to a solicitation package.

opportunity—A future event, that should it occur, would have a favorable impact upon the project.

opportunity assessment—Examination of the uncertainty associated with the possible occurrence of an event that is expected to have a positive impact on a project.

optimizing level—See *maturity level.*

organization—The parent organization of the acquisition organization.

organization's measurement program—The set of related elements for addressing an organization's measurement needs. It includes the definition of organization-wide measurements, methods and practices for collecting organizational measurements and analyzing data, and measurement goals for the organization.

orientation—An overview or introduction to a topic.

periodic review—A review that occurs at specified regular time intervals. See *event-driven review* for contrast.

(risk) plan—A process for determining what, if anything, should be done with a risk. It produces an action plan for individual or sets of related risks. Planning answers the questions:
- Is it my risk? (responsibility)
- What can I do? (approach)
- How much and what should I do? (scope and actions)

probability—The likelihood the risk will occur. Probability is one of the three attributes of a risk. The assessment of a probability may be expressed in Qualitative or Quantitative terms.

policy—A guiding principle, typically established by senior management, that is adopted by an organization or project to influence decisions.

prime contractor—An individual, partnership, corporation, or association that administers a subcontract to design, develop, and/or manufacture one or more products.

procedure—A written description of a course of action to be taken to perform a given task [IEEE-STD-610].

process—A set of activities performed for a given purpose (e.g., the software acquisition process).

process capability—The range of expected results that can be achieved by following a process. See *process performance* for contrast.

process capability baseline—A documented characterization of the range of expected results that would normally be achieved by following a specific process under typical circumstances. A process capability baseline is typically established at an organizational level. See *process performance baseline* for contrast.

process descriptions—Documentation that specifies, in a complete, precise, verifiable manner, the requirements, design, behavior, or other characteristics of a process. It may also include the procedures for determining whether these provisions have been satisfied.

process measurement—The set of definitions, methods, and activities used to take measurements of a process and its resulting products for the purpose of characterizing and understanding the process.

process performance—A measure of the actual results achieved by following a process. See *process capability* for contrast.

process performance baseline—A documented characterization of the actual results achieved by following a process. A process performance baseline is typically established at the project level, although the initial process performance baseline will usually be derived from the process capability baseline. (See *process capability baseline* for contrast.)

project—An undertaking that is focused on acquiring a specific product. The product may include hardware, software, and services. Typically, a project has its own (*product objectives,*) funding, cost accounting, and delivery schedule.

program manager / project manager—1. The role with total business responsibility for an entire project. 2. The individual who directs, controls, administers, and regulates a project acquiring software, a hardware/software system, or services. The project manager is the individual ultimately responsible to the end user.

program office / project office—The aggregate of individuals assigned the primary responsibility for acquisition in the contracted effort. A project office may vary in size from a single individual assigned part time to a large organization assigned full time.

project risk—See *risk.*

project's defined acquisition process—See *acquisition process.*

qualitative assessment—The probability is stated in qualitative units such as; none, low, medium and high.

qualitative attributes—See *attributes*

quantitative assessment—A numeric analysis of risk estimates including probability of occurrence to forecast the project's schedule and cost using probabilistic data and other identified uncertainties to determine likely outcomes.

quantitative control—Any quantitative or statistically-based technique appropriate to analyze a acquisition process, identify special causes of variations in the performance of the acquisition process, and bring the performance of the acquisition process within well-defined limits.

quantitative level—See *maturity level*

repeatable level—See *maturity level*

required training—1. Training required by the organization, 2. Mandatory training for the organization to acquire the appropriate knowledge and skills to initiate and sustain project and organizational processes and objectives. See *training* for contrast.

reserve—See *management reserve*

risk—The possibility of a future event, should it occur will have an effect on project objectives including cost, schedule or technical. The effect could be positive, in which case the project manager has an opportunity to improve project performance or mitigate risk. Often, however, the effect is adverse to the objectives. The source of the risk can be identified and often its likelihood of occurring and impact on the project objectives quantified. The process of risk identification and assessment is to turn "unknown unknowns" (uncertainty) into known risks for the purpose of better managing the project.

risk analysis—The process of combining and studying the effects of multiple risk assessments to better understand important project issues such as: the mean effect of risks, min/max exposures, risk prioritization, sensitivity analysis, etc. A given analysis tends to provide a "snapshot" in time of the project's risk environment. A risk analysis is often done with a *Monte Carlo* simulation. The simulation is based on risks which are identified and quantified as probability distributions at a detailed level of the project such as the activity level of a schedule or a low-level WBS cost element. The simulation combines the probability distributions of uncertain results at the detailed level using a model of the project, such as a critical path schedule. Results derived include (1) the probability of meeting the project objective such as a completion date, (2) the contingency needed to achieve an acceptable level of likely project results, and (3) the location within the project of the risks which put the objective in greatest jeopardy."

risk assessment—1. The process of estimating the *probability* and *impact* for each risk identified to ensure that they are understood and can be prioritized, 2. The review of identified risks to see if they are acceptable according to proposed actions.

risk attitude—An organization or person's attitude toward risk. Risk neutrality may be defined as making decisions based on the expected value of alternative actions, such as a large company with many projects or an insurance company may do. Risk aversion is common, however, among organizations for which the impact of the risk is substantial (e.g., bankruptcy, loss of a prized customer) and extra contingency may be required in this case. Some organizations are risk seekers; they will not act to minimize risk but may expose themselves to risk, relying on crisis management in reaction to risks that actually occur.

risk database—A database for risks associated with a project.

risk driver—The technical, programmatic and supportability facets of risk.

risk event—An occurrence that may affect a project, positively or negatively.

risk exposure—The impact of a risk multiplied by its probability of occurring.

risk identification—The process by which events which could affect the project objectives are identified and described. Their base causes (not symptoms) are identified and described, indicators are specified that will warn of their occurrence, mitigation steps in the current plans are detailed, their owners are listed for future action, and their impacts are discussed. Risk identification is conducted by people familiar with the project and potentially others knowledgeable from experience with similar projects or independent expertise. Identification and quantification are often accomplished in the same interview.

risk management—1. The process associated with identifying, analyzing, planning, tracking, and controlling project risks, 2. The lifecycle process which includes identification, assessment and analysis, but adds the identification and implementation of proactive actions which are intended to mitigate risks and enhance opportunities. The management process also includes monitoring the efficacy of planned actions and the continuous update of all assessments as they change due to the implementation of actions and/or changes in the project environment with the passage of time.

risk management plan—The detailed project planning which is required to incorporate and new activity into the overall project plan. The estimated cost is derived directly from the *risk management plan*. As described for *impact*, the cost estimate may be qualitative or quantitative and if quantitative may be probabilistic in nature. The risk management plan has its own risks, too. No plan is free of risk.

risk management strategy—See *risk management plan*

risk set—grouping of like risks within the same WBS level for analysis.

risk statement—Statement of condition and consequence to define the uncertainty and impact of an event.

role—Defined responsibilities that may be assumed by one or more individuals.

solicitation package—When seeking suppliers for a particular acquisition, it is the information distributed which tells the interested bidders what the requirements are, how to prepare their proposals, how proposals will be evaluated, and when to submit their proposals. Sometimes called Request for Proposals (RFP).

standard—Mandatory requirements employed and enforced to prescribe a disciplined, uniform approach to development or acquisition.

standard acquisition process—See *acquisition process*

statement of work (SOW)—Narrative description of products or services to be supplied under contract that states the specifications or other minimum requirements; quantities; performance dates, times and locations, if applicable; and quality requirements.

tailor—To modify a process, standard, or procedure to better match (project) process or product requirements.

technology—The application of science and/or engineering in accomplishing a particular result.

task—A well-defined component of a project *activity*.

total installed cost *(of a project)*—All capital cost plus client furnished materials.

track—A process in which risk data are monitored by the person(s) responsible for tracking watched and mitigated risks. Tracking risks includes three activities:

- acquiring tracking data
- compiling tracking data
- reporting tracking data

(*project*) **training**—Training for project personnel to acquire appropriate knowledge or awareness to initiate and/or sustain project specific processes and objectives. (See *required training* for contrast).

uncertainty—A situation in which only part of the information needed for decision-making is available.

unplanned benefit—An automatic benefit accrued if an opportunity actually occurs. Examples include: increase in incentive payment, unanticipated sales, improvement in team morale, etc. This benefit is typically one component of an opportunity impact.

variance—The difference between the baseline and the current expected value.

work breakdown structure (WBS)—A deliverable-oriented grouping of project elements that organizes and defines the total scope of the project. Each descending level is an increasingly detailed definition of a project component, which may be products or services.

Index